hot & hip
HEALTHY
GLUTEN-FREE
COOKING

hot & hip
HEALTHY
GLUTEN-FREE
COOKING

75 Healthy Recipes to Spice Up Your Kitchen

WRITTEN AND PHOTOGRAPHED BY
BONNIE MATTHEWS

Skyhorse Publishing

Visit our website at www.skyhorsepublishing.com.

10 9 8 7 6 5 4 3 2 1

Library of Congress Cataloging-in-Publication Data is available on file.

Jacket design by Anna Christian
Cover photo by Bonnie Matthews

Print ISBN: 978-1-63220-291-8
Ebook ISBN: 978-1-63220-752-4

Printed in China

For Kenny Reed and Anne Marie Aristone Gallagher, friends and trainers, who helped spark in me a passion for fitness that will never burn out.

Special thanks to Arabella Girardi, for helping behind the scenes with so many of the cookbooks, with words and with her passion for food. Also special thanks to my friends and neighbors, Kelli Felix, Nancy Ortega, and Alysia Gadson, who helped create, cook, taste test recipes, and make an occasional late-night run to the grocery store!

Contents

Introduction

A Little Bit About Me

I'm hoping you've picked up this book for several reasons. One, to be inspired by mealtime options as opposed to being stressed about what's for dinner. It seems like so many people I know stress over what to have for their next meal, when really just a little planning ahead can allow free time to actually enjoy cooking and the process of prepping for meals. I know for myself, I do really enjoy cooking and had to relearn how to cook and prepare foods for health a few years ago. You see, I had to lose weight, and though I didn't do it through gluten-free foods, I did do it with healthy meal planning and cooking simple, delicious meals that included ancient grains. Grains in general, I feel, have gotten a bad rap lately in the media. But to me they are an excellent vehicle to add texture, fiber, and proteins to one-pot meals and salads. For me, the style of cooking I created as a busy self-taught cook was to go for big flavor and go for stuff that will last in the fridge a few days to portion out meals.

My personal 130-pound weight loss was a result of several factors, which included not eating out often or eating a lot of prepared foods, and making meals at home. And, of course, teaching my body to work for me so that I wasn't working for it. I learned how to make my body burn fat through lifting weights and doing interval training. And the meals I prepared were delicious and also functional. I knew that I was not going to be able to drop 130 pounds just by drinking some green juice or eating protein bars—that was just not my path, nor did it seem like something I'd be able to sustain in my life. By discovering ways to prepare easy meals that included high protein, high fiber grains, and homemade dressings, I didn't feel I was sacrificing my pleasure of food. In fact the opposite occurred! My "Me Project" became an incredible lesson in discovering a newfound love of food. All foods! Vegetables, vinegars, fish, etc. Grains, of course, were an integral part of that. My time at the gym and in the kitchen was and still is an important part of my day and is essential in maintaining my weight loss and overall health.

Gluten-free Lifestyle vs. Gluten-free as a Necessity
Even if you don't have to live a gluten-free lifestyle, incorporating gluten-free foods into your diet is a great way to add more variety, flavor, and fun to mealtimes. There are so many gluten-free grains that are delicious and easily available in stores and online nationwide; whether you are gluten-free or not, they are worth trying for variety and for health. It's also a golden opportunity to try some awesome ancient grains like amaranth, an eight-thousand-year-old grain that was once a staple food of the Aztecs.

Allison Massey, MS, RD, LDN, CDE of Mercy Medical Center in Baltimore, says, "Higher fiber and protein grains are excellent to incorporate into one's diet. They aid in satiety, or that feeling of fullness, which is helpful for individuals working towards weight loss or healthy weight maintenance." I know for a fact that feeling full helped me lose a ton of weight with ancient grains. "Each grain type we consume, gluten-free or not, contains varying nutrients, so it's healthy to include a wide variety of whole grains to reap the benefits of different vitamins, minerals, and phytochemicals," says Lauren Harris-Pincus, MS, RDN.

Why settle for brown rice when you can serve teff, sorghum, arrowroot, sago, and other delicious options? This book is filled with unique and intriguing recipes containing grains that are just as easy to prepare and a heck of a lot more interesting. Use these recipes as a launchpad to more satisfying meals that will please your palate, keep your waistline happy, and make mealtime a reason to celebrate.

So What the Heck is Gluten Anyway?
Gluten is the elastic protein in wheat, rye, and barley. It's the stuff that gives bread that wonderful chewy texture. It's the "glue" that keeps foods, like your favorite bakery treat, from becoming a crumbly mess. For some it can be very difficult to digest. Others have a sensitivity to it that can cause digestive issues. Some people are actually allergic to it.

How does "gluten-free" taste? Foods without gluten don't have that flaky, doughy, fluffy texture, but they offer new flavors and textures plus the chance to impress your friends and family with a decidedly different menu, including ancient grains they've never heard of or tasted. Purple cauliflower pizza crust anyone? In some cases, there's no grain at all in the recipe. Just veggies and other foods.

Many (not all, but some) of the gluten-free cookbooks I've seen on the market are focused mainly on baked goods. While that's really important, since wheat flour is a huge part of baking and substitutions need to be available, my cookbook has a large focus on dinner meals, quick lunches, and hors d'oeuvres, not just baked goods. My hope is that you'll get your taste buds excited about the recipes and will want to explore other grains to add to your meals. And for you foodies out there, my hope is you'll learn about unusual rice like black rice, mahogany rice, Bhutan red rice, sprouted jasmine rice . . . not the old humdrum brown rice. And to discover great new gluten-free pastas that are on the market now, like the Explore Asian® spaghetti, made with organic adzuki beans, and their Mung bean and edamame fettuccine. They are both very flavorful and loaded with protein and fiber. They are a great vehicle to use as a base for adding all kinds of vegetables and layers of flavor to any quick meal.

What Foods Contain Gluten?
Gluten is commonly found in wheat and foods containing wheat. Think bread, pasta, crackers, cookies, flour tortillas, and cakes. Sneaky gluten can also turn up in foods you wouldn't expect like candy, salad dressing, soy sauce, and lunch meat.

The good news is, the market is exploding with gluten-free fare, so there are plenty of tasty, gluten-free substitutes out there for you to try. Be warned, however! "Most packaged 'gluten-free' products are full of refined flours made with stripped down rice and corn and loaded with refined sugars and hydrogenated oils," according to Lauren Harris-Pincus. She says that many of the store-bought gluten-free baked goods have far worse nutritional stats than their gluten-containing counterparts. How do you find healthy choices? Read the labels! Look for products that contain whole grains, like sorghum, oats (certified gluten-free), quinoa, kañiwa, amaranth, buckwheat, millet, teff, and, of course, a wide variety of rice grains mentioned previously. They have higher protein and fiber and taste delicious.

Why Are So Many Americans Giving Up Gluten?

Advocates claim that a gluten-free diet can ease a number of ailments, including digestive problems, eczema, chronic fatigue, headaches, ADHD, autism, and diabetes. Some of these people may be allergic or sensitive to gluten and may feel better by avoiding it. Still others just perceive a gluten-free diet to be healthier.

Many of the gluten-free products in the marketplace can often be higher in carbohydrates and calories than non-gluten-free choices. "Remember gluten-free, fat-free, and sugar-free aren't necessarily giving you the 'green light' that the product is a good choice; it's still important to look at the label and see if it's the right choice for you," says Allison Massey.

In the last two years it seems as though gluten-free diets have become trendy, and they've received the "'healthy halo' and uninformed individuals assumed that just because a product was gluten-free it was healthy which is not necessarily true," according to Massey. One more reason to make some foods at home using ingredients you've read about and in which you trust the nutrition.

As many as three million people in the United States have no choice but to avoid gluten altogether. These people have celiac disease, a digestive disorder that damages the small intestine so that it can't do a good job of absorbing nutrients from your food. It can lead to rapid weight loss and even malnutrition if left untreated.

Still others have a gluten sensitivity and in fact may have a "larger sensitivity with digesting larger groups of foods that contain FODMAPs (fermentable oligosaccharides, disaccharides, monosaccharides and polyols)," Massey says. Gluten is a FODMAP and can aid in abdominal discomfort and can be a challenge to digest. For those folks, it's beneficial to avoid foods containing gluten and foods containing FODMAP.

Whether you need to live a gluten-free lifestyle or you're looking to add more variety to everyday eating, this book offers a good place to start. The possibilities are endless. Have fun playing and exploring some of these awesome ancient grains. Now quit reading and get cooking.

Chapter 1: Batter Up Breakfast Solutions

Almond Orange Muffins with Goji Berries and Teff Flour

Makes 12 muffins
Preheat oven to 350 degrees F.

1 cup teff flour

½ cup Bob's Red Mill gluten-free general baking flour

½ cup almond flour/meal

¾ cup coconut sugar

2 teaspoons baking powder

½ teaspoon baking soda

½ teaspoon ground cinnamon

¼ teaspoon pink salt

2 large eggs

¾ cup milk or almond milk

2 tablespoons fresh-squeezed orange juice

½ teaspoon vanilla extract

¼ cup coconut oil, liquid

1 cup goji berries (with a few extra for the top of muffins)

Zest of 1 large orange

½ cup slivered almonds (with a few for the top of muffins)

2 drops orange oil flavoring (if you don't have it, skip it)

Line muffin tin with paper muffin liners.

In a large bowl, whisk together teff flour, general baking flour, almond flour, coconut sugar, baking powder, baking soda, cinnamon, and salt.

In a separate small bowl, whisk eggs, milk, orange juice, vanilla extract, and coconut oil until blended.

Stir egg mixture into the flour until combined. Gently add in goji berries, orange zest, almonds, and orange oil flavoring.

Spoon the batter into the lined muffin tin about three-quarters full. Top with a few extra almonds if desired.

Bake about 25 minutes, or until a toothpick inserted in the center of a muffin comes out clean.

Blueberry Pancakes with Amaranth, Quinoa, and Almond Flour

Makes about 5 4-inch pancakes

¾ cup amaranth flour

½ cup quinoa flour

½ cup hazelnut flour (or almond flour)

1½ tablespoons arrowroot powder

3½ tablespoons coconut sugar

1½ teaspoons ground cinnamon

½ teaspoon cardamom, ground

½ teaspoon pink salt

2 eggs, whisked

1 cup almond milk

½ teaspoon vanilla extract

1 tablespoon coconut oil, melted
  (plus a little more for the skillet)

1 cup fresh or frozen blueberries, thawed

Top with grade B maple syrup or honey

In a large bowl, combine the first eight ingredients.

Stir in the remaining ingredients until mixed through.

In a separate bowl, whisk eggs, almond milk, vanilla, and coconut oil together, then add to the dry ingredients. Mix with spoon. Fold in blueberries. Add a tad more liquid if it seems too stiff. It can be thick, but not too stiff.

Heat up about 2–3 teaspoons of coconut oil in a skillet over medium heat. Spoon in the batter to make a pancake about 4 inches wide or less. Cook about 3–4 minutes per side and flip when the edges become brown.

Serve immediately with a little honey or maple syrup.

Savory Kañiwa Frittata with Yam and Goat Cheese

Makes 4 servings

If you have any leftover cooked grains, this is the perfect recipe to use them in. If not, you can cook some.

½ cup kañiwa grain

1 cup vegetable broth or water

½ onion, chopped

1 medium yam or sweet potato, shredded
(skins on are OK)

2 large garlic cloves, smashed, minced

2–3 tablespoons cilantro, chopped

A few dashes of pink salt

2 dashes of cayenne pepper

Fresh black pepper to taste

5 eggs

½ cup goat cheese, crumbled
(or feta cheese)

Drizzle of extra virgin olive oil

Coconut oil for the skillet

A handful or two of arugula

Top with fresh arugula that's been
seasoned with olive oil and pink salt

In a medium saucepan, toast the dry kañiwa with a drizzle of olive oil. Stir in 1 cup vegetable broth or water and bring to a boil, then reduce to a simmer. Cook until the water is absorbed—about 15 minutes, stirring frequently to prevent sticking. You can tell it's done when the "spiral-like" germ sprouts out of the grain and becomes visible. Once done, let stand covered for 2–3 minutes and fluff with a fork before continuing.

In a separate skillet, sauté the vegetables and garlic in olive oil. Add in cilantro, salt, cayenne, and black pepper. Cook vegetables until tender and set aside when done.

In a medium bowl, whisk eggs and cooked grains and stir in all other ingredients.

Using the same skillet that the vegetables were sautéed in, add a drizzle more of olive oil and heat over medium-high heat. Pour the mixture into the skillet and cook covered a few minutes until the edges become browned. Carefully take a spatula and release the edges of the frittata from the skillet edge and flip the frittata over. Cook further about 3–5 minutes. Slice and serve with arugula that's been dressed with extra virgin olive oil and pink salt. Top with a bit more goat cheese and black pepper if desired.

Note: If you have any extra kañiwa left over, pop it in your freezer and have it available for an egg scramble for another day.

Hearty Muffins with Pepita Seeds, Raisins, Oats, Flax, and Sorghum Flour

Makes about 12
Preheat oven to 400 degrees F.

½ cup almond meal

½ cup quick-cook oats

¼ cup + 2 tablespoons sweet rice flour

½ cup sorghum flour

½ cup tapioca starch

½ cup coconut sugar

½ teaspoon xanthan gum

1 tablespoon baking powder

1½ teaspoons cinnamon

½ teaspoon pink salt

¼ cup flax seeds

¼ cup coconut oil, liquid (or butter)

2 eggs

1 teaspoon vanilla extract

1–1¼ cup almond milk or regular milk

1 cup raisins

Top with ½–1 cup pepita seeds

In a medium bowl, combine first eleven ingredients.

In a separate small bowl whisk together wet ingredients and then add them to the dry ingredients. Add in raisins and stir until just moistened.

Spoon into greased muffin tin or lined muffin tin about three-fourths full. Top with pepita seeds or a little coconut sugar.

Bake for about 18–20 minutes or until a toothpick inserted in the center of a muffin comes out clean.

Breakfast Lasagna with Vegetarian Chorizo Crumbles

Makes one 9 x 13 casserole dish
Preheat oven to 350 degrees F.

You can use browned chorizo sausage or vegan sausage crumbles that are gluten-free. I used Tofurkey Chorizo Crumbles® for mine. They are seasoned really nicely.

1 package gluten-free vegetarian
  sausage crumbles
2 cloves garlic, smashed and minced
1 sweet red pepper, chopped
1 small onion, chopped
½ cup of fresh cilantro, chopped
1 teaspoon mild chili powder or fajita
  seasoning
8 eggs
Pink salt and generous amounts of fresh
  black pepper to taste
8-ounces fresh baby spinach,
  roughly chopped
2 cups nonfat cottage cheese
Cooking spray for casserole dish
About 8–10 gluten-free lasagna noodles
  (cooked to al dente); look for fresh or
  dry that you don't have to cook first
1 16-ounce jar medium or mild salsa
½ cup crumbled goat cheese
Option: For spicier flavor, add a half
  a jalapeño that's been seeded and
  minced. Mix that into onion mixture.

In a skillet heat up vegetarian chorizo crumbles or diced-up regular chorizo over medium heat. After about 3–4 minutes add in garlic, red pepper, onion, ¼ of the cilantro, and chili powder. Cook further until peppers and onions are tender. Set aside.

In a large bowl, whisk eggs with pink salt and fresh cracked pepper. Mix in spinach and rest of the cilantro and cottage cheese.

In a greased 9 x 13-inch baking dish, place 4 lasagna noodles along the bottom. Pour in the egg and cottage cheese mixture. Then add a layer of the chorizo mixture. Top again with a layer of noodles. Pour the salsa over the top. Top with a little crumbled goat cheese. Cover with tinfoil.

Bake covered with tinfoil for about 35–40 minutes. Then remove tinfoil and bake further for about 10–15 minutes, or until a knife inserted in the center comes out clean.

Once done, allow to set about 10 minutes prior to cutting. Garnish with minced cilantro.

Other options: Top with thin slices of fresh tomatoes before baking.

Mexican-style Egg Cups with Gluten-free Spinach Petals

Preheat oven to 400 degrees F.

8 eggs

2 teaspoons medium chili powder

1 teaspoon onion powder

½ teaspoon cumin

1 cup onions, diced

1½ cups canned pinto beans or black beans, rinsed and drained

1 cup cherry or grape tomatoes, quartered and pat dry

1 jalapeño or fresno pepper, seeded, minced

½ cup cotija cheese or queso fresco

1 cup cilantro, chopped

1 clove garlic, smashed and minced

1 package Gluten-Free Tortilla Petals®— either the spinach or red chimayo red chili kind*

In a large bowl, whisk eggs and add in chili powder, onion powder, and cumin. Then stir in all remaining ingredients except for the gluten-free tortilla petals.

Spray muffin tin with cooking oil and then rip tortilla petals and line the muffin tins with the pieces. Pour in ingredients about three-fourths full.

Top with a little more cheese and diced tomato if desired.

Bake about 25 minutes or until an inserted knife comes out clean. Allow to cool 3–4 minutes prior to removing from muffin tin. Top with diced cilantro if desired.

***Note:** You can substitute any gluten-free tortilla wrap if you can't find these. Look in the bread section or even the freezer section for selections.

Banana Pancakes with Hazelnut and Quinoa Flour Topped with Cocoa Nibs

These are thick hearty pancakes! Add more dates if you like.
Makes about 8–10 medium pancakes

2 eggs

½ teaspoon vanilla

1½ cups almond milk or milk

2 teaspoons melted butter or ghee,
  cooled

1½ cups quinoa flour

½ cup hazelnut flour

2 teaspoons baking powder

2 teaspoons coconut sugar

Dash of pink salt

2 ripe bananas, smashed

Toppings: honey or grade B maple syrup,
  options to top with vanilla nonfat Greek
  yogurt and flax seeds

Optional toppings: chopped hazelnuts or
  chopped pecans, coconut oil or walnut
  oil for cooking (or any kind of oil), ¼ cup
  cocoa nibs or chopped chocolate pieces

In a large bowl whisk eggs, vanilla, milk, and butter.

In a separate bowl mix flours, baking powder, coconut sugar, and salt. Add the wet ingredients to the dry and stir until moist. Add in bananas until just moist.

Heat coconut oil in a skillet on medium heat. Add about ¼ cup of batter into the skillet for each pancake. Cook until bubbles form around the edges or until edges are slightly crisp. Then flip and cook further about 2–3 minutes.

Breakfast Sage Burger with Bhutan Red Rice, Rainbow Chard, and Asiago Cheese

Serve with fruit, coffee, and an egg on top
Makes 6–8 4-inch burgers

About ½ cup of gluten-free Chorizo sausage crumbles

¾ cup vegetable broth or water

About ⅓ cup Bhutan red rice (or other rice)

1 cup canned chickpeas, rinsed, lightly mashed

2 large eggs, lightly beaten

⅓ cup teff flour

1 cup red chard, chopped—main vein removed first

1 cup carrots, grated

2 garlic cloves, smashed, minced

½ cup asiago cheese or manchego cheese, grated

2 tablespoons olive oil

¼ teaspoon pink salt

¼ teaspoon pepper

2 teaspoons sage, fresh diced or ground

½ teaspoon smoked paprika

Fresh cracked pepper to taste

Grapeseed oil for cooking

In a skillet over medium heat add a drizzle of extra virgin olive oil. Brown the sausage crumbles and drain any oil once done.

In a small saucepan add ¾ cup broth and rice and bring to a boil. Cover, reduce heat, and simmer for about 30 minutes until tender.

In a large bowl, whisk eggs, add in cooked sausage, rice, and all remaining ingredients. Stir thoroughly. If it seems too dry, add a little olive oil. If it seems too moist, add a little more teff flour. Add fresh cracked pepper.

For best results allow mixture to chill in the refrigerator about 30 minutes.

Form patties with your hands using about ½ cup of the mixture. Flatten them slightly with the palms of your hands—about 1 inch thick. Heat grapeseed oil over medium-high heat. Add the patties carefully to the pan using a spatula. Cook about 5 minutes per side or until they are crisp and golden.

Top with additional rainbow chard that's been dressed with olive oil if desired—along with a little more grated asiago cheese. Or if you really want to make it fancy, cook some fresh whole sage leaves in a little olive oil and garnish with that instead.

Breakfast Hash with Sweet Peppers, Brussels Sprouts, Japanese Yams, and Sorghum

Makes 4 servings

Preheat oven to 375 degrees F.

Note: The sorghum takes about 50–60 minutes to cook, so you may want to make this the day before breakfast time rolls around.

1 medium yam or sweet potato, diced and roasted (I used a yellow Japanese yam)

About 1½ cups brussels sprouts, shaved and roasted

¾ cup sorghum grain

2½ cups vegetable broth

½ onion, chopped (or use leeks)

½ sweet red bell pepper, chopped

½ sweet yellow bell pepper, chopped

6–8 fresh cremini mushrooms

4–5 dried porcini mushrooms, rehydrated in water

Olive oil

Pink salt and fresh black pepper

Optional: Drizzle a little balsamic glaze in for a brighter flavor.

Spray cooking oil on a baking sheet. Place diced sweet potatoes and brussels sprouts on the sheet and add salt and pepper. Spray a little cooking oil on top and cook in oven for about 15 minutes or until tender.

Rinse sorghum and drain. Then add sorghum and 2½ cups vegetable broth to a saucepan. Over medium heat, bring to a boil. Cover, reduce heat to low, and let simmer until tender—about 50–60 minutes. Drain any excess water.

In a large skillet, add a drizzle of olive oil and heat up on medium. Add in onion, bell pepper, and mushrooms and cook until tender. Toss in roasted sweet potatoes and brussels sprouts. Add in pink salt and fresh black pepper to taste.

Serve with eggs and fresh fruit, if desired, and a side of baby mixed greens dressed with white balsamic.

Other options: For heartier protein options, add in Beyond Beef Crumbles®. They are vegan and found in the refrigerator section. Or for a nonvegan alternative, add in diced browned Applegate® chicken apple sausage—both are really flavorful.

Egg Cups with Hot Smoked Salmon

Makes 12 muffins (freeze some!)
Preheat oven to 375 degrees F.

These little egg cups are a fantastic portable high protein breakfast that can be made ahead of time. I also love them after a workout with salad for a light lunch. You can use any kind of hot smoked salmon you can find. It can often be found in vacuum-packed pouches in the seafood section of the grocery store. Or use leftover grilled salmon from home. I used Trader Joe's Hot Smoked Peppered Salmon, and it's wonderful on top of salads too.

To add variety to this recipe, add in sautéed mushrooms, sweet bell peppers, or diced kale.

12 eggs
¼ cup diced fresh basil
½ cup crumbled goat cheese
1–2 cups fresh spinach or baby kale, diced
A few dashes of garlic powder
A few dashes of onion powder
¼ teaspoon fresh black pepper
Pink salt or sea salt
8–10 gluten-free tortilla wraps (I used the Rudi's Fiesta Gluten-Free Tortilla wraps—look for them in the freezer case)
About 1 cup of hot smoked salmon, crumbled into chunks

In a large bowl, whisk the eggs. Add in the basil, goat cheese, diced kale, and spices.

Spray two muffin tins with cooking spray. Take the tortilla wraps and rip them into thirds—making uneven strips. Line the muffin tin with the wraps, making sure the entire bottom is covered with tortilla. Fill each nearly to the top, leaving room for the salmon. The tortilla wraps can extend beyond the height of each muffin hole. Once all the cups are filled, add a few pieces of salmon to each muffin tin and poke them into the egg mixture. Place them in the oven for about 15–20 minutes or until a knife or toothpick inserted near the center of the muffin comes out clean and dry.

KHAO DENG RUBY
RED RICE

TRI-COLORED QUINOA

MILLET

KAÑIWA

THAI STICKY PURPLE RICE

AMARANTH

Chapter 2: With the Grain

Curried Garbanzo Beans with Eggplant and Brown Basmati Rice

Makes 4 servings

Preheat oven to 450 degrees F.

1 cup brown basmati rice

2 cups water or vegetable broth

1–2 tablespoons extra virgin olive oil or ghee (or butter)

1 teaspoon cumin seeds

1 medium eggplant, cut into ½-inch cubes with skins on

1 yellow onion, chopped

1 14-ounce can fire-roasted tomatoes

1 15-ounce can garbanzo beans, rinsed and drained

2 garlic cloves, smashed and minced

½-inch fresh ginger root, minced fine (or grated fine)

1 tablespoon medium curry powder

1 jalapeño pepper, seeded and minced

Pink salt and pepper to taste

Garnish with fresh cilantro, chopped

Fresh lemon for garnish

For the Rice:
Place brown basmati rice and water or vegetable broth in a medium saucepan. Cook on high until boiling. Reduce and simmer with lid on for about 20–25 minutes or until tender. In a skillet, add about 1 tablespoon of olive oil or ghee and heat on medium. Add in about ½ teaspoon of cumin seeds and heat through. Mix into rice after rice is done.

For the Eggplant:
Lightly coat diced eggplant with olive oil and toss onto a baking sheet. Cook in preheated oven for about 20 minutes. Once done, remove and set aside.

For the Curry:
Heat olive oil or butter in a skillet over medium heat. Add in remaining cumin and onions. Cook onions until translucent and slightly brown.

Add in tomatoes, garbanzo beans, garlic, ginger, and curry. Cook for about 2–3 minutes.

Add roasted eggplant and jalapeño pepper and cook further for about 10–15 minutes.

Serve family style on a platter with the rice. Top with chopped fresh cilantro and lemon wedges.

Seafood Stew with Edamame and Mung Bean Fettuccine

Makes 6 servings

¼ cup extra virgin olive oil

2 medium onions, thinly sliced

2 tablespoons dried Greek oregano

½ teaspoon freshly ground black pepper

⅛ teaspoon cayenne

4 teaspoons red wine vinegar
   (if you don't have it, skip it)

½ cup white wine (optional)

3 cups vegetable stock or fish stock

Generous pinch of saffron threads

3–4 large garlic cloves, smashed and
   minced

2 cans fire-roasted tomatoes in garlic and
   basil (or plain)

2 pounds fish fillets, try any combo of the
   following: orange roughy, mahi-mahi,
   black cod, scallops, shrimp (shells
   removed)

1 bunch curly kale, deveined, or latticino
   kale (dinosaur kale), chopped into
   bite-sized pieces, deveined if desired

About ½ package Explore Asian® edamame
   and mung bean fettuccine pasta

In a large saucepan over medium-high heat, sauté the onions in olive oil until they just begin to brown. Stir in the oregano, pepper, and cayenne, if desired.

Add the vinegar and white wine (if using) and let the mixture boil until the vinegar has evaporated a little bit. Stir in stock, saffron, and garlic and bring the mixture to a boil. Add the tomatoes.

Bring the stew to a boil. Add the fish fillets and kale and reduce to low.

While that is cooking, cook pasta according to package instructions and set aside once done.

Simmer soup for about 15 minutes further and serve over cooked pasta.

For Crostini:
Preheat oven to 350 degrees F.

Slice your favorite multigrain gluten-free bread into long strips and drizzle or brush with a little extra virgin olive oil. Sprinkle with sea salt or pink salt. Place on a baking sheet and cook in preheated oven for about 15–20 minutes until crisp.

Three Leaf Salad with Pistachios and Lemon Dressing

Makes 2 servings
Preheat oven to 375 degrees F.

20–30 red seedless grapes

1 small container of grape or cherry
tomatoes

¾ cup brown rice (or about 1½ cup fully
cooked brown rice)

½ cup raw or roasted pistachios,
chopped

About 4 tablespoons raw hemp seeds
(or use flax seeds or chia seeds)

A handful of each of these greens—or
enough to make 2 salads:
Fresh baby spinach
Fresh basil leaves
Fresh arugula, baby or regular

Shallot vinaigrette

4 tablespoons extra virgin olive oil or
pumpkin seed oil

About 1 tablespoon shallot, minced fine

1½ teaspoons honey

1½ teaspoons honey mustard
(nongrainy style)

3 tablespoons apple cider vinegar

2 tablespoons white balsamic vinegar
(or skip this and just use 5 tablespoons
apple cider vinegar)

2 large cloves garlic, smashed and
minced

½ teaspoon onion granules

Grapes and Tomatoes:
In a large bowl, toss grapes and tomatoes with a little olive oil. Place them on a baking sheet and roast for about 15–20 minutes or until they are just blistering but not completely popped. Once done, remove and allow to cool.

Once cooled, toss all ingredients and serve with fresh cracked pepper. For more protein, add some store-bought roasted chicken.

Spicy Black Bean Noodle Salad with Cabbage and Thai Peanut Sauce

Makes 6 servings

Serve chilled

1 package Explore Asian Organic Black
    Bean Spaghetti®

½ head small cabbage, shredded
    (or substitute 2 packages of pre-
    shredded slaw mix for the 2 cabbages)

2 cups fresh sugar snap peas, or snow
    peas, cut in half

½ head small purple cabbage, shredded

1 package shredded carrot

1–2 small cans Mandarin orange
    wedges, drained

1–1½ cups Thai peanut sauce (I like
    San-J® brand because it has a nice kick)

4 teaspoons toasted sesame seed oil
    (or more if desired)

Optional: Add ¼ cup seasoned rice
    vinegar for extra tang.

1 bunch fresh cilantro, diced (including
    the stems)

1 cup sliced almonds (or substitute
    chopped peanuts or cashews)

Cook pasta according to package instructions, then remove from heat and place in a large bowl to cool.

While noodles are cooking, shred the cabbage, and dice the vegetables. Mix them in a large bowl with a spoon. Add the peanut sauce, toasted sesame seed oil, and rice vinegar if you are using it. Mix gently. Gently stir in noodles, cilantro, and nuts.

Serve room temperature or chilled.

Best Ever Garlicky Croutons with Super Simple Fast Salad

For the Croutons:

Makes about 4 cups of croutons

Preheat oven to 350 degrees F.

¼ cup of good quality extra virgin olive oil

3–4 fresh large garlic cloves, smashed and minced

4–5 slices of your favorite multigrain gluten-free bread, cut into ½-inch cubes with crust.

A few dashes of sea salt or pink salt

Optional: About a teaspoon of dried Italian seasoning or herbes de' Provence.

Prior to cooking the croutons, add the garlic to olive oil and allow to sit covered at room temperature for at least an hour or more. This will allow the olive oil to infuse with the peppery garlic. Believe me, it's worth the wait if you can leave it for even three hours.

In a large bowl, toss in the bread cubes and drizzle the olive oil over them, stirring occasionally to coat evenly.

Once coated, transfer them to a large skillet and cook over medium heat until the edges are slightly browned. Add a few dashes of salt and a few cranks of fresh pepper while they cook. Stir often. If the bread you are using is firm and dense, you can simply remove from the skillet and allow to cool without placing in the oven to crisp up. They often will get more crisp as they cool down and dry. However, if the bread you use is lighter, once golden, place them on a cookie sheet and cook in the oven to dry out for about 5 minutes. Watch them carefully so they don't burn. Once done, allow to cool on top of the stove and serve on your favorite salad.

Note: They can be eaten right away or stored in an airtight container in the refrigerator for a day or two. If they get soggy, simply place them back in the oven to crisp them up.

For the Super Simple Fast Salad:

Fresh smashed garlic

Extra virgin olive oil or pumpkin seed oil—yum!

Fresh squeezed lemon

Mixed baby greens or baby romaine lettuce

Radishes, sliced

Raw sunflower seeds

Store-bought rotisserie chicken or Applegate Farms® all natural turkey or chicken lunch meat

For the dressing, just smash a little garlic into some olive oil and squeeze in some fresh lemon. Mix thoroughly. No vinegar needed! In a bowl, toss in baby lettuces or arugula and slivered radishes. Add a few sprinkles of raw sunflower seeds and toss in the croutons. If you want to make it a complete meal with more protein, just toss in some leftover cooked chicken or diced chicken or turkey. I really like Applegate Farms® because it is organic and all natural—it doesn't contain any nitrates or nitrites. In fact, their turkey slices only contain turkey, water, and spices! That's a no brainer.

Black Bean and Quinoa Pasta with Fresh Grilled Tomato, Basil, and Pine Nuts

Makes 4 servings
Preheat oven to 375 degrees F.

These noodles made by Ancient Harvest® are so delicious—really one of the best gluten-free pastas I've tasted! Some folks may be skeptical due to their unusual color—but they are worth trying, not only for flavor but also because they are nutrient dense as compared to some of the quinoa pastas that are blended with corn. With this pasta, weighing in at 7 grams of fiber and 12 grams of protein, it's a winner!

2 cups cherry or grape tomatoes

Drizzle of extra virgin olive oil

1 8-ounce box of Ancient Harvest® Bean and Quinoa elbow pasta

3–4 garlic cloves, smashed and minced

2 teaspoons butter or ghee

1 cup pine nuts

2–3 teaspoons or more of good quality parmesan cheese

About ½ cup goat cheese

2 cups fresh basil leaves, loosely chopped

A few cranks of fresh cracked black pepper

A pinch or two of pink salt or sea salt to taste

Toss tomatoes in a bowl with a little olive oil to coat. Place on rimmed baking sheet and roast until slightly blistered, about 15–18 minutes. Then set aside.

Cook noodles according to package instructions.

In a large skillet, heat a drizzle of olive oil over medium-high heat. Add in garlic and stir quickly so garlic gets golden but does not burn. Just as it begins to get golden, add in roasted tomatoes—including skins. Cook for about 2–3 minutes. Add in 2 teaspoons butter or ghee. Add in pine nuts, cheeses, and basil. Stir gently and serve immediately with additional fresh cracked pepper and salt to taste.

Forbidden Rice Salad with Heirloom Carrots and Cauliflower

Makes about 6 servings
Preheat oven to 375 degrees F.

Serve this warm

2 cups vegetable broth or chicken broth

1 cup black forbidden rice or
   mahogany rice

2 tablespoons butter

1½ cups heirloom cauliflower, chopped
   (I used yellow, green, and purple
   varieties)

2 heirloom carrots, sliced into thin coins
   (use any kind of carrots)

1 leek, white part sliced

About ¼ fresh fennel bulb, with some
   fennel tops set aside

Extra virgin olive oil or walnut oil

Pink salt and fresh cracked black pepper
   to taste

2½ teaspoons sumac

2 garlic cloves, smashed and minced

1 cup canned chickpeas, rinsed and
   drained

Options: Add about 1 teaspoon of
   Bragg's Liquid Aminos® to vegetables
   prior to roasting.

In a medium saucepan, bring water or vegetable broth and rice to a boil over high heat. Reduce, add 2 tablespoons butter, cover, and simmer for about 25 minutes or until tender.

Toss cauliflower, carrots, leek, and fennel into a bowl and drizzle a little olive oil. Add in a few pinches of salt and pepper. Add about ½ teaspoon of sumac and the garlic and stir to coat.

Place vegetables on a baking sheet and roast in preheated oven for about 15–20 minutes or until tender.

Once vegetables are done, toss them in a skillet with the chickpeas. Drizzle in a little olive oil and a little more water or vegetable broth. Add in remaining sumac. Cook for about 5 minutes and remove from heat. Mix in cauliflower and serve with chopped fresh fennel tops and a bit of fresh black pepper.

Moroccan Rice with Beef, Dried Fruits, and Nuts

Makes 4–6 servings
Preheat oven to 375 degrees F.

2 small or 1 large red yam, diced and
   roasted (I left skins on)
Extra virgin olive oil
1¼ pounds beef
   (I used round cut, diced)
1½ teaspoon allspice, ground
¾ teaspoon cinnamon, ground
¼ teaspoon cardamom, ground
3 cloves of garlic, minced fine
1½ cups beef broth, or water
½ cup Bhutan red rice, uncooked (or
   brown jasmine rice)
4–5 dried apricots, chopped
4–5 dates, seeded and chopped
2–3 strips of lemon peel, or pickled lemon
Pink salt and pepper to taste
2–3 teaspoons honey
¼–½ cup pistachios, pine nuts, or slivered almonds
A little fresh mint, chopped (optional)

For the Red Yam:
Chop up the red yam with skins on and toss it in a little olive oil. Place on a baking sheet lined with parchment paper (if you have it). Cover lightly with tinfoil and cook for about 25 minutes or until fork tender. Once done, remove and set aside.

For the Beef and Rice:
Dice the beef in small bite-sized pieces. Drizzle a little olive oil in a large skillet and heat up over medium heat. Once the meat is browned on all sides, add in the spices, broth, and the rice and raise heat to high. Bring to a boil and then lower heat and cover. Add in apricots, dates, and lemon peel. Allow to simmer for about 25 minutes or until rice is tender. Once the liquid is evaporated and the rice is tender, add salt and pepper to taste. Add in the yam, honey, and nuts. Stir gently and top with mint.

Serve immediately!

Grilled Miso and Orange Tuna Kabobs with Mahogany Rice

Makes 2–3 servings

This recipe requires marinating for up to 3–4 hours for best flavor.

For the Tuna:
1 tablespoon miso paste
2 teaspoons toasted sesame seed oil
4 tablespoons lime juice
4 tablespoons orange juice
4 tablespoon coconut sugar or raw sugar
1 teaspoon fresh grated ginger
2 teaspoon orange zest
¼ teaspoon cayenne pepper
1 teaspoon minced garlic
2 ahi tuna steaks cut into cubes

For the Rice:
½ cup mahogany rice, or black rice
1 cup vegetable broth or chicken broth

For the Veggies:
2 tablespoons toasted sesame seed oil
   (or hot garlic oil instead of this and
   garlic)
2 cloves fresh garlic, smashed and
   minced
3–4 carrots, julienne cut
About 1½ cups sugar snap peas, whole
3–4 green onions, julienne cut
Dash or two of cayenne pepper
Sesame seeds for garnish

Optional: Add about ½ cup broccoli
   crowns.

Marinating the Ahi:
In a small saucepan, combine miso paste, sesame seed oil, lime juice, orange juice, coconut sugar, fresh ginger, orange zest, cayenne pepper, and garlic. Cook marinade on medium heat, stirring constantly. Remove from heat once sugar has dissolved. Allow marinade to cool. Add marinade to medium bowl or resealable bag and add ahi steaks. Mix to coat thoroughly. Store in refrigerator for 3–4 hours.

Grilling the Kabobs:
Prior to grilling, remove the tuna from the refrigerator and allow to sit at room temperature for about 5–10 minutes. Thread tuna onto metal skewers.

Preheat gas grill on high with lid closed; if using charcoal grill, prepare for direct heat cooking over hot charcoal.

Carefully coat the grill surface with cooking spray, spraying at an angle. Add the skewers directly over heat. For well-done ahi steaks, cook for about 4–5 minutes on each side or until internal temperature reaches 145 degrees. Remove from grill and allow to stand for about 5 minutes before serving.

For the Rice:
In a small saucepan bring broth and rice to a boil. Cover, reduce heat, and simmer for about 20–25 minutes or until tender. Then set aside.

For the Veggies:
In a skillet or wok, heat up sesame seed oil and garlic on high. Quickly toss in vegetables and stir in seasonings. Cook just until tender but still crisp.

Toss vegetables with rice. Top with the kabob and serve immediately.

Roasted Beet Salad with Cannellini Beans, Pistachio, Sorghum, and Goat Cheese

Makes 6 servings
Preheat oven to 375 degrees F.

Sorghum is a wonderfully delicious hearty grain and shows off nicely in cold salads and soups. On its own, it's got a great texture and slightly nutty flavor. It does take a little more time to cook than some rice and other grains, but it's worth the effort! It's been a staple for countries in Africa for thousands of years. It's got a strange name and is also called Milo by some brands.

2–3 cups fresh beets with skins on, scrubbed and diced (about 6–8 beets)

A few tablespoons olive oil

1 cup vegetable broth

½ cup raw sorghum, or about 1 cup cooked

1 15.5-ounce can of cannellini beans, rinsed and drained

A few teaspoons apple cider vinegar

Roasted pistachio nuts or roasted pepita seeds (green pumpkin seeds)

Salt and cracked pepper to taste

About ½ cup crumbled nonfat feta cheese or nonfat goat cheese

A few fresh basil leaves, chopped rough

For the Beets:
Scrub the beets thoroughly, removing the stems, leaves, and any roots. Cut beets into bite-sized cubes and place them on a tinfoil-covered baking sheet. Drizzle a little olive oil on top and bake on the middle rack in the oven. Cook for about 30 minutes or until tender. Remove from oven and let cool to room temperature.

For the Sorghum:
Pour broth and sorghum in a saucepan and bring to a boil, cooking for 1 minute. Reduce heat to low. Cover and simmer for about 40–50 minutes until sorghum is tender. While it's cooking, do not let the saucepan run out of water. Add a little while cooking if necessary until the grain is tender. Let the sorghum cool before making the salad.

Assembling salad:
Toss all ingredients together except for cheese and basil. Mix gently, then add cheese and basil. Serve chilled. Add more apple cider vinegar if desired.

Note: In a hurry? Skip the sorghum and replace with fully cooked brown jasmine rice or brown rice—found in the grocery aisle. Many stores carry this now and also have it available in the freezer case, fully cooked! Also look for fully cooked beets in vacuum-packed containers in the produce shelves. A popular brand to ask for is Mellissa's Organics®. This is a fast timesaver for a party and requires zero cooking!

Forbidden Rice® Ramen with Shrimp and Miso Soup

Makes 2 servings

In a hurry for a fast meal? Look for Forbidden Rice® Ramen Miso Soup made by Lotus Foods. It only takes 4 minutes to cook and you can add other ingredients for unlimited variations for quick soup bowls to pop in your bag for work!

1 package Forbidden Rice® Ramen with
   Miso Soup by Lotus Foods

About 6–8 fully cooked de-shelled shrimp

About 1 cup fresh baby spinach

2 cups water

About a ½ teaspoon sriracha sauce or
   red chili and garlic paste

In a medium saucepan, place 2 cups water and bring to a boil. Add noodles and reduce heat to low. Simmer for about 4 minutes, stirring occasionally. When noodles are just softened, add in fully cooked shrimp and spinach and the packet of seasoning that comes with the noodles. Once the spinach is wilted in the soup, serve immediately with the sriracha sauce stirred in.

Swiss Chard and Artichoke Salad with Cannellini Beans and Bhutan Red Rice

Swiss Chard and Artichoke Salad:

2 cups cooked Bhutan red rice

1 12.5 ounce can cannellini beans, rinsed and drained

½ red bell pepper, seeded and diced

½ cup kalamata olives, pitted and sliced

12–14 grape or cherry tomatoes, sliced in half

About 6–8 large leaves of Swiss or rainbow chard, deveined and chopped

About 10 marinated artichoke hearts (look for them on the salad bar)

Pink salt and fresh cracked pepper to taste

Basil Dressing:

Makes about ¼ cup of dressing. Double if you want extra for another day. Keeps in the fridge for up to 5 days.

½ cup extra virgin olive oil

2 heaping teaspoons tahini

A dash or two of salt

Dash of cayenne

Fresh black pepper

6 tablespoons fresh lemon juice

1 teaspoon lemon zest (or more if desired)

3 large garlic cloves, smashed and minced

6–8 fresh large basil leaves, loosely chopped

In a food processor, mix all dressing ingredients. Taste test and adjust if you want more lemon or garlic or peppery finish.

Toss all salad ingredients together. Drizzle dressing over and toss. Serve with more lemon if desired.

For added crunch, add spiced pepita seeds—look for them in the bulk section of some grocery stores.

Fast and Savory Chicken Soup with Quinoa, Brown Rice, and Mushrooms

Makes 4–5 servings

1 32-ounce package chicken broth
  (I like Pacific Free-Range Organic
  Chicken Broth®)

2 carrots, diced (skip the peeling)

2 cloves garlic, smashed and minced

1 teaspoon fresh thyme

½ teaspoon fresh diced sage

½ teaspoon fresh chopped rosemary

1 handful cremini mushrooms

1 package dried medley of mushrooms
  (or about 2 ounces dried porcini
  mushrooms, rehydrated)

1 whole rotisserie chicken, store-bought,
  fully cooked

1 cup marsala wine, or cooking sherry

2 8.5-ounce packages Seeds of Change®
  Organic Quinoa and Brown Rice with
  Garlic packages (fully cooked in the
  grocery aisle)

1 small onion, chopped

Pink salt and fresh black pepper to taste

In a large pot, add broth and heat over medium-high heat, covered. Add in carrots and seasonings and cook for about 10 minutes. Add in mushrooms and reduce to simmer on low-medium.

Remove skin and bones from chicken and discard them. Toss chunks of chicken into soup and cook further for about 10–20 minutes on low heat. Add in marsala wine. Add in fully cooked rice.

For a thicker soup, remove some of the carrots and blend in a food processor with some of the broth and add back into the soup. Add more salt and pepper to taste.

Serve immediately.

Roasted Carrots and Parsnips with Za'atar and Forbidden Rice

Makes 3–4 servings
Preheat oven to 450 degrees F.

I've included Bragg's Liquid Aminos® in this recipe. If you've never tried it, it's a great gluten-free substitute for soy sauce, which contains gluten. Bragg's Liquid Aminos has 16 essential and nonessential amino acids—all naturally occurring. It adds a great taste to veggies or fish. Use it as a flavor enhancer as you would a soy sauce. It comes in a jar or spray bottle too!

1 cup vegetable broth

½ cup forbidden rice

½ pound parsnips, peeled and cut into about 2-inch pieces

½ pound carrots, peeled and cut into about 2-inch pieces

2 tablespoons extra virgin olive oil

½ cup edamame, frozen and shelled

2 teaspoon za'atar seasoning

1–2 teaspoons Bragg's Liquid Aminos®

Pink salt and fresh cracked pepper to taste

In a saucepan heat vegetable broth and rice over medium-high heat. Bring to a boil, then cover and reduce heat to low. Simmer for about 20 minutes or until tender and water is evaporated.

Toss parsnips and carrots in a bowl and coat lightly with olive oil. Toss onto a rimmed baking sheet and season with fresh cracked pepper and a few shakes of salt. Roast for about 20 minutes or until they are tender and slightly golden. Stir about halfway through cooking.

Place edamame in a bowl with a few tablespoons of water. Cover with a paper towel and cook in the microwave for about 3–4 minutes or until they are warm and tender.

Once done, toss all ingredients together with za'atar seasoning and serve. Add in more Bragg's Aminos or za'atar seasonings to taste.

Zesty Kañiwa Salad with Roasted Vegetables and Basil Vinaigrette

Makes about 4 servings
Preheat oven to 375 degrees F.

If you have been gluten-free for years, you definitely have tried quinoa by now. Well, kañiwa is a smaller red cousin to quinoa that is becoming more widely available in bulk bins and on store shelves. Look for it in the grain section of natural food stores. The good thing about kañiwa is that you don't have to prewash the grain as you do sometimes with quinoa. And the grain itself is so small you can cook some ahead and keep it in the fridge to toss in salads or egg scrambles any time you are looking to add in more protein and fiber.

For the Salad:

3 carrots, chopped (I used heirloom red and yellow ones)

1 cup fresh green beans

2 cups water or vegetable broth

1 cup kañiwa grain (makes about 2½ cups cooked grain)

8–12 green Castelvetrano olives, pitted and chopped*

½ pint grape tomatoes

6 fresh mozzarella pearls, cut into small pieces (either marinated pearls or plain)

1 6–8 ounce bag of fresh arugula

Extra virgin olive oil or cooking oil

For the Basil Vinaigrette:

Makes about 1 cup of dressing

½ cup plus 2 tablespoons extra virgin olive oil

1 cup white balsamic vinegar

5 large garlic cloves, smashed, minced

15–18 large basil leaves, loosely chopped

Fresh cracked pepper

Pink salt to taste

The Vegetables:

In a large bowl, toss carrots and green beans. Toss them onto a baking sheet and roast for about 15–20 minutes or until desired tenderness is reached. I like them slightly crunchy for this recipe. Toss tomatoes in olive oil and roast on a separate sheet for about 10–15 minutes or until they are just blistering but not completely popped. Once done, remove and allow to cool.

The Kañiwa:

In a medium saucepan over high heat, bring vegetable broth and kañiwa to a boil. Add a few pinches of salt. Reduce to low heat, cover, and simmer until all the water is absorbed—about 15 more minutes, stirring occasionally. You will know the grain is fully cooked when spiral-like germ becomes visible. Remove from heat and allow to stand covered for about 2–3 minutes.

In a large bowl toss cooled kañiwa, green beans, carrots, and olives with some of the dressing, stirring gently. Add fresh cracked pepper. Gently stir in tomatoes. Serve on top of fresh arugula greens with additional dressing to drizzle over top.

The Basil Vinaigrette:

Mix all ingredients in a food processor until smooth. Add more vinegar and salt to taste. For a thicker dressing, add a little avocado or plain nonfat Greek yogurt.

*Castelvetrano olives are large, bright green buttery fruity olives. They are not fermented like some olives, so they retain their bright green appearance. They are often found in salad bars where other Mediterranean foods are located, or look for them in jars in the grocery aisle.

Hearty Southwestern Chicken Veggie Soup with Bean and Quinoa Pasta

Serves 8

½ to 1 cup (or about 1½ cups when cooked) Ancient Harvest® black bean and quinoa elbow pasta (or other gluten-free pasta)

2 chicken breasts, skinless, boneless, cut into cubes

4 cups chicken broth

1 cup medium-spiced store-bought salsa

1 tablespoon extra virgin olive oil

1 medium onion, diced

½ jalepeno, seeded, diced (more or less to taste)

1 14.5-ounce can fire-roasted tomatoes in green chilies (look for them, they are awesome!)

1½ cups tomato juice or V-8 juice

2–3 medium carrots, sliced (skip the peeling)

2 tablespoons freshly squeezed lime juice

1 cup fire-roasted corn (in freezer case) or regular frozen corn kernels

3 teaspoons ground cumin

1 teaspoon medium chili powder

1 teaspoon ancho powder (if you don't have add ½ jalapeño, seeded and diced)

1 teaspoon oregano

4 garlic cloves, smashed and minced

½ teaspoon pink salt

½ cup chopped cilantro

1 medium zucchini or medium yellow squash, or pattypan squash, cut into ½-inch chunks

Options:

Additional fresh cilantro

Dollop of plain nonfat Greek yogurt (or Mexican Crema)

Cook pasta according to package instructions and set aside.

Place all ingredients except zucchini and pasta in a large pot. Cover and cook for about 15–20 minutes over medium heat, stirring occasionally. Add zucchini and cook further for about 5–8 minutes. Serve over pasta in bowl and toss extra cilantro on as garnish. Optional: add a dollop of nonfat Greek yogurt on top.

Vietnamese Salad with Grilled Shrimp and Purple Yam Noodles

Makes 4 servings

10–14 medium raw shrimp, shelled
  (or use frozen, thawed, fully-cooked
  shelled shrimp)
½ package of purple yam vermicelli
  (about 8 ounces)*
1 cup carrots, julienne sliced
1 cup fresh basil (or Thai basil), chopped
½ to 1 cup fresh mint, chopped
½ to 1 cup fresh cilantro, chopped
4 green onions, chopped, include the
  white part and some of the green stem
2–3 red fresno peppers, seeded, thinly
  sliced depending on desired heat
  (use red or green jalapeños as a
  substitute)
4 tablespoons coarsely chopped unsalted
  roasted peanuts

For the Dressing:

1½ tablespoons brown coconut sugar, or
  turbinado sugar
⅓ cup seasoned rice vinegar
2–3 tablespoons red chili garlic paste
1 tablespoon fresh lime juice
2 tablespoons fish sauce
1½ tablespoons sesame oil
1 tablespoon light sodium soy sauce
  (optional)

For the Shrimp:
Heat a cast iron skillet on high heat. Add a little cooking spray and cook shrimp on each side, turning once, for about 1 minute per side, or until firm and pink. Once done, remove and set aside.

For the Noodles:
Bring a large pot of water to boil over high heat. Once boiling, turn heat off and add the noodles. Stir slightly to separate the noodles. Let stand for about 5–7 minutes or until the noodles are tender to the bite yet not soggy. Remove and place in a colander. Rinse with cold water and drain.

For the Dressing:
Mix the coconut sugar and rice vinegar together and heat in the microwave for about 10–13 seconds to melt the sugar. Then add that to a large bowl along with the other dressing ingredients and stir well. Taste test and decide if you want more or less heat. If you want more tangy taste, add 1–2 more tablespoons of fresh lime juice.

Final Step:
Add the noodles to the dressing and stir to coat. Tongs work better for this than a spoon. Add the diced vegetables, herbs, noodles, and shrimp. Stir to coat. Add the fresno peppers to the top of the bowl or simply toss in.

If desired, add a few more chopped peanuts to the top of the bowl for a nice presentation. Serve immediately.

*If you can't find the yam vermicelli, substitute thin rice noodles, or look for Thai Kitchen® Purple Corn and Rice Noodles. Cook these the same way as the recipe.

Chapter 3: Flatbreads, Pizzas, and Wraps

Grilled Panini with Fire-Roasted Pepper and Goat Cheese

Makes 1 sandwich

Sandwiches can be a blessing and a curse for folks trying to eat healthy. Often when eating them at a café, you have no idea what the quality of ingredients are or how much butter or fat they are using to grill the sandwich.

So why not make them at home instead?

Here's a super fast way to make an awesome café-quality panini.

2 slices of your favorite multigrain or seeded gluten-free bread

A few slices of frozen grilled zucchini and eggplant, thawed (or make your own on the grill)

A slice or two of fire-roasted sweet red or yellow pepper (look for this in a jar near the pickles at the store)

About an ounce of goat cheese, or your favorite low-fat cheese

Cracked pepper and sea salt or pink salt to taste

Ghee, butter, or Earth Balance® vegan spread

Options: For more protein, add a few slices of good-quality all natural chicken or turkey.

Heat up a cast iron griddle skillet or regular skillet on medium-high heat.

Coat the pan with a very small amount of the butter you are using. Assemble the sandwich with all the ingredients except the butter. Place the sandwich on the griddle and smash it down with the bottom of another heavy skillet or use a metal spatula. Once the edges begin to brown, carefully turn the sandwich over and brown the other side.

Eat immediately! Serve with a nice salad or some healthy sweet potato and beet chips.

Fast Lunch: Mexican Wrap with Chicken and Chipotle Hummus

Makes 2 servings or more

About 1 cup store-bought rotisserie chicken, diced

½ cup Vegenaise® or mayonnaise

1 chipotle in adobo sauce, chopped (in a can, in the ethnic section of the store)

2 gluten-free tortillas (I like the Gluten-Free Sandwich Pedals—Red Chimayo variety, or use any gluten-free tortillas)

1 small package shredded cabbage or slaw cabbage medley (or about 2 cups shredded cabbage from the salad bar)

½ mango, diced

¼ cup cilantro

Lime wedges

About ½ cup store-bought red pepper hummus (or plain hummus)

A few dashes of pink salt

Dice store-bought rotisserie chicken and place in a bowl with Vegenaise® and mix in half of the chipotle. Add in a little of the sauce from the can as desired for heat and flavor. Toss in shredded cabbage, diced mango, cilantro, squirts from 2 lime wedges, and a dash of salt. Gently stir, but not too much.

In a small bowl, mix in the other half of the chipotle and the hummus. Mix thoroughly.

Smear the mixture on the gluten-free tortilla wrap. Top with the chicken and slaw mixture. Add sliced avocado and serve either open-faced or rolled up. Garnish with additional lime if desired.

Fast Lunch: Curried Flatbread with Chicken and Hot Curry Paste

Serve hot or cold
Makes 2 servings or more

About 1 cup store-bought rotisserie chicken, diced (or diced all natural chicken lunchmeat)

2 teaspoons Vegenaise® or mayonnaise or plain nonfat Greek yogurt

¼ cup cilantro

About 4 teaspoons purple onion, minced

1 small ataulfo mango, diced (or any kind of ripe mango)*

2 gluten-free tortillas (I like the Gluten-Free Sandwich Petals)

2–4 butter lettuce leaves or romaine lettuce

2–3 teaspoons Hot Curry Paste**

Optional: ½ red bell pepper, diced
Optional: If you have any leftover cooked sweet potatoes or yams, dice them up and toss in with the chicken too.

Dice store-bought rotisserie chicken and place in a bowl with Vegenaise®.

In a medium bowl, mix the eggplant relish with Vegenaise®. Add in cilantro, purple onion, and the chicken and gently stir, but not too much. Add mango and a dash of salt if desired.

Heat the tortilla wrap in a skillet with a little cooking spray, ghee, or olive oil. Heat through on each side.

Remove from heat and place each one on a plate.

Add a few lettuce leaves onto the tortilla wrap.

Divide the curried chicken mixture evenly and place on top of the lettuce.

Serve open-faced or rolled up.

NOTE: If desired, add a tiny bit of the Vegenaise curry mixture onto the heated tortilla before adding the lettuce and chicken.

* If you can't find a ripe mango, skip it—the frozen kind has no flavor.

** Look for Patak Binjal Eggplant Relish®—it's widely available in the ethnic food section of many grocery stores. If you can't find it, substitute mild curry paste or another spicy condiment like harissa paste. Look for it near the hummus in the refrigerator case or in the grocery aisle near other Mediterranean foods.

Purple Cauliflower Pizza with Sundried Tomatoes and Cilantro Pesto

Makes 2 9-inch personal-size pizza crusts
Preheat oven to 425 degrees F.

Cauliflower can be found in four colors–white, and three heirloom varieties: yellow, green, and purple. They taste all about the same to me, but it is fun to play with the other colors to change up recipes.

For the Crust:
4 cups purple cauliflower (or any kind), grated or chopped fine
1 large egg, lightly beaten
1¼ cups shredded part-skim mozzarella cheese
⅓ cup parmesan cheese, grated (or pecorino romano)
½ teaspoon dry oregano
4 tablespoons chickpea flour (or other gluten-free flour)
½ teaspoon garlic powder
A few dashes of pink salt and pepper to taste

For the Toppings:
3–4 medallions goat cheese (more or less to taste)
1 cup sundried tomatoes (packed in olive oil)
½ cup Kalamata olives
½ teaspoon crushed red pepper flakes

For the Cilantro Pesto:
Makes about 1 cup
1 whole bunch of cilantro
½ cup olive oil
½ cup pine nuts or walnuts, loosely chopped
2 large cloves garlic, loosely chopped
1 whole lemon, juiced
Pink salt and pepper to taste
A dash or two of cayenne

Place parchment paper on a rimmed baking sheet.

Grate cauliflower. Place about 2 cups of the crumbles in a large bowl and cover with a paper towel. Microwave with about 3 tablespoons of water for about 3 minutes. Stir and cook for a few more minutes or until soft. Remove and allow to cool slightly.

In a bowl, mix the egg, mozzarella, and parmesan. Then add the cauliflower, oregano, chickpea flour, garlic powder, and salt and pepper, and stir until ingredients are evenly distributed. Once mixed, divide mixture in half on the parchment paper and flatten out to about 9-inch circles. If you don't have parchment paper, simply spray a baking sheet with cooking spray generously before adding the cauliflower to the tray.

Top pizza crusts with the goat cheese and cook for about 10–12 minutes. Then add the sundried tomatoes, Kalamata olives, and red pepper flakes. Cook further about 8–10 more minutes or until the edges of the crust begin to get browned and the goat cheese begins to melt. Remove from oven and top with drizzles of cilantro pesto.

For the Pesto:
Combine all ingredients in a food processor until blended well. Spoon onto pizza once cooked, or if you have a plastic squeeze bottle, use that to drizzle onto the pizza.

Tuna and Lemony Artichoke Pizza with Capers and Manchego Cheese

Makes 2 flatbread pizzas
Preheat oven to 375 degrees F.

1 9-ounce jar marinated artichokes,
   drained and sliced in half
About 4–6 teaspoons manchego cheese,
   grated, or parmesan cheese
Dash of red chili flakes
2 cloves garlic, smashed and minced
Juice from 2–3 lemon wedges
1 teaspoon extra virgin olive oil
2 gluten-free tortilla wraps
1 can Tongol Tuna packed in water or oil,
   drained (or Tonnino tuna)
2–3 teaspoons capers
6–7 Castelvetrano olives, pitted, chopped
   (look for them on the salad bar—they
   are very bright greenish blue)
Dash of pink salt
Fresh cracked pepper
Microgreens or pea sprouts to top

Optional: Finely sliced purple onion
Fresh flat-leaf parsley, cilantro, or basil to
   garnish

Place half of the jar of artichokes in a food processor with the cheese, red chili flakes, garlic, and a dash or two of pink salt and black pepper. Pulse until just loosely blended. Add in lemon juice and about 1 teaspoon of extra virgin olive oil and pulse just 2 or 3 more times, then remove.

Place in a bowl and add in sliced onion, if using. Taste and adjust as desired for more lemon or salt.

Place two tortilla wraps on a baking tray that has been coated with cooking spray, or place tortillas on top of parchment paper on the tray. Spread the artichoke mixture over each tortilla. Sprinkle crumbled tuna, capers, and olives overtop. Add any remaining artichokes on top.

Bake in oven for about 20–25 minutes and top with microgreens or other small chopped greens.

Serve warm.

Curried Salad Wrap with Grapes and Walnuts

Makes enough for 2–3 wraps
Preheat oven to 350 degrees F.

1 small to medium red yam or sweet
   potato, diced with skins left on

2 teaspoons extra virgin olive oil

Pink salt to taste

1 package precooked quinoa and brown
   rice (found in the grocery aisle)

2 teaspoons mild curry powder, or use
   Patak's® Mild Curry Paste

3–4 teaspoons Vegenaise® or
   mayonnaise

2–4 teaspoons nonfat Greek yogurt

½ granny smith apple, diced (skins can
   stay on if desired)

About ½ cup slivered almonds or
   walnuts, chopped

About 10 red seedless grapes, sliced and
   quartered

2–3 gluten-free tortilla wraps

Optional: Fresh cilantro or frozen, thawed
   peas added in

Place yam in a bowl and drizzle on extra virgin olive oil on to coat lightly. Add a pinch of salt. Stir and pour onto a baking sheet that's either lined with parchment paper or tinfoil. Cover with tinfoil and bake for about 15–20 minutes or until just tender. Be careful not to overcook—they shouldn't be mushy.

While the yam is cooking, using the same bowl, add in the precooked quinoa and brown rice mixture and curry powder. If you are using Patak's Mild Curry Paste®, mix that in a separate bowl with the Vegenaise® and nonfat Greek yogurt first, then mix it into the rice.

Add in Vegenaise®, Greek yogurt, apple, almonds, and grapes, gently stirring to coat.

Once the yams are done, remove from the oven and allow to cool.

Toss them into the bowl of ingredients and stir to coat. Adjust seasoning as desired. Toss in fresh cilantro and/or thawed frozen peas if desired.

Place on tortillas and eat rolled up.

Other options: for additional moisture and flavor, make a little extra sauce blending the yogurt, curry paste, and Vegenaise® and serve a dollop on the side with each wrap.

Fast Chicken Wrap with Red Pepper Hummus

Serve cold
Makes 2 servings or more

2 gluten-free tortilla wraps

¼ cup store-bought red pepper hummus

1 carrot, julienne cut or get shredded
carrot from the salad bar

About 3 tablespoons purple onion,
sliced finely

3–4 tablespoons banana peppers (from
jar, diced)

5–8 slices of all natural chicken or turkey
lunch meat (Applegate Farms® has
organic)

Pea sprouts, broccoli sprouts, or any kind
of your choice

3–4 teaspoons Vegenaise® or mayonnaise (optional)

Butter lettuce or other lettuce leaves
of choice

Optional: For an added spicy kick, blend
a little harissa into the red pepper
hummus.

Lay the tortilla wrap flat on a plate; spread red pepper hummus evenly.

Add shredded carrot, purple onion, and banana peppers. Top with slices of chicken. Add a little Vegenaise® or mayonnaise. Add a little salt and pepper. Top with sprouts and lettuce. Wrap up and eat!

Thai Flatbread Pizza with Shrimp and Peanut Sauce

Makes 2 flatbread pizzas
Preheat oven to 375 degrees F.

Serve with shredded cabbage slaw on the side with rice vinegar, peanut sauce, and diced peanuts.

1 teaspoon toasted sesame seed oil or extra virgin olive oil

About 4 teaspoons red bell peppers

A few slivers of purple onion

8 medium-large precooked shrimp from the fish counter

1–2 teaspoons Bragg's Liquid Aminos® (tastes similar to soy sauce but it's gluten-free)

2 gluten-free tortilla wraps

About ¼ cup San-J Thai Peanut Sauce® (it is gluten-free!)

2–3 tablespoons roasted almonds, cashews, or peanuts, chopped

3–4 teaspoons fresh cilantro, loosely chopped

2–3 teaspoons of sesame seeds

For the Slaw:

About 2 cups red and white cabbage mixed or store-bought shredded cabbage package

About 3 tablespoons Vegenaise® or mayonnaise

Dash of cayenne pepper

Dash or two of pink salt

1 teaspoon seasoned rice vinegar or mirin (either is fine)

3–4 tablespoons cilantro, loosely chopped

For the Flatbread Pizzas:

In a small skillet, heat sesame seed oil. Once it's really hot, add in peppers and onion. Cook for about 3 minutes and stir often. Toss in precooked shrimp and cook for just a minute with the Bragg's Liquid Aminos®.

Remove from heat. Place two tortilla wraps on a parchment paper–lined baking tray. Spoon on the peanut sauce to coat evenly. Arrange the peppers and onions and place the shrimp evenly on each tortilla.

Bake in oven for about 20–25 minutes. Top with peanuts, cilantro, and sesame seeds.

Serve with a generous portion of Asian slaw.

For the Slaw:

Mix all ingredients together and serve.

Makes about 2 cups of slaw (enough for 2 servings).

Buffalo Chicken Flatbread Pizza

Makes 2 personal-sized pizzas
Preheat oven to 375 degrees F.

This recipe will vary depending on the brand of ingredients you have available to you. But no matter what, it's a great, fast go-to meal for lunch or dinner. The kids will love this one!

2 chicken breasts, fully cooked

2 flatbread Sandwich Pedals® Chimayo Red Chile variety (or any kind of gluten-free tortilla)

About ¼ purple onion, cut julienne

About ½ cup crumbled goat cheese or blue cheese

Louisiana hot sauce or buffalo sauce you enjoy (or a red bbq sauce)

A few sprigs of cilantro, loosely chopped

For the Chicken:
Use store-bought cooked chicken breasts and cut into strips or make your own: coat deboned, skinless chicken breast with a little extra virgin olive oil, pink salt, and chipotle powder or mild chili powder. Spray a little cooking spray on a baking sheet and place chicken on top.

Cook for about 25 minutes or until internal temperature reaches 165 degrees F. Once cooked, slice into strips and set aside.

For the Pizza:
Place flatbread or tortillas on a greased baking sheet.

Top with chicken, onion, and goat cheese, and bake for about 12 minutes or until the onions begin to brown and the goat cheese begins to melt slightly. Remove from oven and add buffalo sauce—as much as desired.

Top with loosely chopped cilantro and serve immediately.

Chicken Salad Wrap with Sumac-Herbed Black Rice

Makes 2 servings
Serve cold or room temperature

½ cup black rice, or mahogany rice blend (look for Lundberg Japonica)

1 cup water or vegetable broth

About 4 ounces rotisserie chicken, chopped, or any kind of fully cooked skinless and boneless

2 teaspoons lemon juice

1 tablespoon extra virgin olive oil

Pink salt and pepper to taste

¾ teaspoon sumac

1 garlic clove, smashed and minced

¼ cup thinly sliced green onion

About 2 tablespoons finely chopped flat-leaf parsley

2 tablespoons, cilantro, chopped

1 tablespoon fresh mint, chopped

½ teaspoon lemon zest

3 teaspoons slivered almonds or pistachios, chopped

Optional: Add your favorite store-bought hummus to the tortilla before filling with the salad.

In a small saucepan over high heat, add rice and water or broth. Bring to a boil, then cover and reduce to simmer about 30–45 minutes or until tender.

Drain excess water if needed. Allow to cool uncovered.

Place chicken in a large serving bowl. Add lemon juice, olive oil, salt, pepper, sumac, and garlic. Let stand about 5 minutes.

Stir in remaining ingredients along with the rice and gently stir.

Divide mixture on top of tortilla wraps and enjoy open-faced or rolled up.

Fast Open-Faced Mediterranean Wrap

Makes 4 servings

Delicious wrap with pesto, feta, lemon, green or black olives, pine nuts, tomatoes, and shredded rotisserie chicken, with rainbow chard and cucumber.

1 teaspoon extra virgin olive oil

½ cup pine nuts, toasted

bout 3 tablespoons lemon juice

1 teaspoon lemon zest

3 teaspoons red wine vinegar

1 tablespoon extra virgin olive oil

1 clove garlic, smashed and minced

½ teaspoon dry oregano (or half if it's fresh)

2–4 teaspoons flat-leaf parsley, minced

2 cups fully cooked grains, cooked in water or broth, cooled

About 1½ cups grape tomatoes, Little Splendito®, or cherry tomatoes

About 2 cups rotisserie chicken fully cooked, diced (or any kind of skinless boneless chicken, diced)

½ cucumber, diced

A ½ cup Kalamata olives, pitted, diced

About 2–4 leaves rainbow chard or kale, deveined and chopped

¼ cup Peppadew red peppers, chopped (look for the roundish red peppers on salad bars)

¼ cup crumbled feta cheese

Pink salt and fresh cracked pepper to taste

2 tortilla wraps

In a small skillet over medium heat, add about a teaspoon of extra virgin olive oil. Add pine nuts and stir constantly. Cook until golden brown; be careful not to overcook. Add a pinch of salt. If skillet is getting too hot, raise the skillet above the flame away from heat and swirl skillet around to circulate the pine nuts. Remove and allow to cool once golden brown.

To make the dressing: In a large bowl, whisk lemon juice, lemon zest, red wine vinegar, olive oil, garlic, oregano, and parsley. Add pink salt and black pepper to taste and set aside. Add diced chicken and allow to marinate about 5 minutes.

Mix all ingredients together except for tortilla wraps and mix gently.

Adjust seasoning to taste.

Place a generous amount of filling on tortilla wrap and roll up to enjoy. Or just eat it on its own without the wrap!

WILD RICE

JAPANESE HATO MUGI
"JOB'S TEARS"

BLACK BEAN PASTA

WEHAM RICE

LENTIL AND QUINOA PASTA

ADZUKI BEAN SPAGHETTI

BEAN AND QUINOA PASTA

FORBIDDEN RICE RAMEN

Chapter 4: Dinnertime Meals

Fast and Easy: Seared Tuna with Edamame and Mung Bean Fettuccine with Peanut Sauce and Sugar Snap Peas

Makes enough for 2 people

1 or 2 tuna steaks

A little toasted sesame seed oil

½ package (uncooked) Explore Asian® Organic Edamame and Mung Bean Fettuccine

1 cup sugar snap peas or snow peas

½ yellow bell pepper, julienne cut

½ red bell pepper, julienne cut

3 spring onions, chopped, including about an inch of the green stem

About ½ cup or more San-J Thai Peanut Sauce® (it's gluten-free)

Optional: Top with chopped cilantro and sesame seeds or chopped roasted peanuts.

Prior to cooking tuna, allow to rest at room temperature for about 10 minutes.

Drizzle a little toasted sesame seed oil in the skillet or, if grilling, directly on the tuna.

Using a skillet or grill, sear tuna steaks on both sides, leaving the center pink if desired for medium rare, or until internal temperature reaches 125 degrees F. Cook further if you want it more well done.

Once done, allow to rest.

In a medium pot, bring about 3 cups water to a boil. Add fettuccine. Reduce heat and simmer gently for about 7–8 minutes or until cooked through.

Once done, drain in a colander and rinse with cold water.

In the same skillet used to cook tuna, add a little more toasted sesame seed oil. Heat on high and add in vegetables and cook for about 3–5 minutes or until they start to get tender. Add in noodles and the San-J Thai Peanut Sauce. Stir to coat and divide onto two plates.

Slice up tuna steaks and fan out on top of the noodles and vegetables. Top with cilantro, sesame seeds, or chopped peanuts.

Gnocchi with Roasted Kabocha Squash, Heirloom Spinach, and Sage

Makes 4 servings
Preheat oven to 400 degrees F.

Kabocha squash is a dark green pumpkin-like squash with pale lines. It's got a very rich creamy sweet flavor when roasted—so sweet you don't even need to add butter or anything to it. Great on its own, but even better when tossed into this recipe. For other options, try using sugar pumpkins when in season. Or if you're in a hurry, look for precut butternut squash in the produce aisle or freezer case of most grocery stores.

1 medium kabocha squash (or 1 package of fresh precut butternut squash*)

A little cooking spray or extra virgin olive oil

1 12-ounce package fresh gluten-free potato gnocchi

4 tablespoons Earth Balance™, ghee, or butter

2 garlic cloves, smashed and minced

1 small pinch nutmeg

About 8 large fresh sage leaves, diced, and a few extra for garnish

¼ cup of vegetable broth or chicken broth

Pink salt and pepper to taste

1 6-ounce bag of heirloom spinach** (or regular baby spinach)

About ¼ cup raw or roasted pepita seeds

*Look for this in the produce aisle.

** Trader Joe's often has a bag of heirloom red spinach for a great price!

For the Kabocha Squash:
Carefully pierce the top of the squash with a large chef's knife and slice squash in half. Remove seeds and fibers and cut into quarters. Coat with cooking spray and place on baking sheet. Cook in preheated oven for about 20 minutes or until just turning tender. Once done and cool enough to touch, peel the skins off with a pairing knife and cut into bite-sized 1-inch chunks.

For the Gnocchi:
Follow package instructions for cooking store-bought gnocchi. Some gnocchi comes fresh in the refrigerator case—other styles can be found in the freezer case or grocery aisle in vacuum-packed packages.

In a large skillet place butter, garlic, nutmeg, sage, and vegetable broth and cook over medium heat. Add in gnocchi, pink salt, and black pepper and stir to coat. Add in squash and the entire bag of spinach. This will be heaping over the skillet at first but will soon wilt down into the skillet. Carefully stir to coat all ingredients.

Once spinach is wilted, toss in pepita seeds. Adjust seasoning to taste and serve immediately.

Almond-Crusted Chicken with Adzuki Bean Spaghetti

Makes 2 servings
Preheat oven to 425 degrees F.

¾ cup almond meal

½ teaspoon dried parsley

¼ teaspoon coarsely ground black
   pepper

¼ teaspoon salt

Dash of cayenne

1 cup yogurt

2 cloves garlic, smashed and minced

2 chicken breasts, skinless boneless

½ package adzuki bean pasta

1 12.5-ounce can fire-roasted tomatoes

4-5 Peppadew peppers, chopped (look
   for them on salad bars—they are bright
   red and roundish)

Flat-leaf parsley or basil for garnish

Mix first five ingredients in a small bowl.

Place yogurt and garlic and a few dashes of salt in a bowl. Add in chicken to coat lightly.

Dip the chicken into the seasoned almond mixture and place on aluminum foil-lined baking sheet.

Top with a little extra dry mixture and pat it down onto the chicken.

Roast for 15–18 minutes until cooked through or reaches 165 degrees F.

While chicken is baking, in a medium pot, bring about 3 cups of water to a boil. Add pasta. Reduce heat and simmer gently for about 7–8 minutes or until cooked through.

Once done, drain in a colander and rinse with cold water.

In skillet, add in tomatoes and Peppadew peppers. Cook over medium-high heat until hot. Add in noodles and stir to coat. Cook further about a minute or two.

Transfer to a plate and top with the chicken.

Garnish with chopped flat-leaf parsley or basil if desired.

Polenta with Fire-Roasted Tomatoes with Green Chili and Cotija Cheese

Makes 6 servings

For the Polenta:

6 cups water

2 cups polenta Bob's Red Mill®
   Polenta Mix

1½ teaspoon pink salt or sea salt

3 tablespoons butter

1 teaspoon chipotle powder

1 teaspoon garlic powder

Extra virgin olive oil or cooking spray

For the Toppings:

1 15-ounce can fire-roasted tomatoes
   packed with green chilies, drained

About ¾ cup of cotija cheese crumbled,
   or queso fresco

Garnish with fresh cilantro and a dusting
   of chipotle powder

In a large, deep pan bring water and salt to a boil over high heat. Slowly add in polenta, stirring frequently. Reduce heat and simmer, stirring frequently to prevent sticking—about 30 minutes. Make sure to use a long-handled spoon to stir as the mixture will bubble up and can burn your hand. Add in butter, chipotle powder, and garlic powder and continue stirring a minute longer.

Oil a deep, medium-sized bowl or lightly coat interior with cooking spray. Spoon polenta mixture into the bowl and allow to stand for about 10 minutes. Once firm, invert onto a flat plate.

It's ready to eat now if you wish to cut it into wedges and top with toppings. Or if you wish to add nice grill marks, cut polenta into wedge shapes and add onto preheated grill that's been coated with cooking spray. Cook covered for about 3–5 minutes per side until nice grill marks occur.

Remove from grill and place on serving tray. Top with the fire-roasted tomatoes, crumbled cotija cheese, and cilantro. Add a few shakes of cilantro powder or mild chili powder on top and serve.

Meatballs with Edamame Mung Bean Fettuccine and Pesto

Makes 2–3 servings

1 pound grass-fed ground beef

4 teaspoons ketchup

About 4 teaspoons onion, minced fine

1 teaspoon garlic powder

2 teaspoons worcestershire sauce

Pink salt and black pepper

A little extra virgin olive oil

½ package Explore Asia Edamame Mung Bean Noodles®

About ¾ to 1 cup fresh store-bought pesto sauce (look for it in the refrigerator case)

About 2 cups fresh baby spinach

6-10 sundried tomatoes, sliced in half

3-4 tablespoons parmesan cheese

2-3 tablespoons crumbled goat cheese

In a medium bowl, add ground beef, ketchup, onion, garlic powder, Worcestershire sauce, salt, and pepper. Mix thoroughly and make into small 1-inch meatballs.

Add a drizzle of olive oil or grapeseed oil to a skillet and heat over medium-high heat.

Once hot, add meatballs and cook until brown on all sides—about 5–6 minutes—or until internal temperature is 165 degrees F. Once cooked, set aside.

In a medium pot, bring about 3 cups water to a boil. Add noodles. Reduce heat and simmer gently for about 7–8 minutes or until cooked through.

Once done, drain in a colander and rinse with cold water.

Add pesto to a large skillet and heat up on medium. Toss in spinach and let it wilt down into the skillet—about 2 minutes. Stir in the noodles, sundried tomatoes, and cheeses and gently stir to distribute sauce and spinach. Toss in meatballs and stir. Serve immediately.

Mushroom Soup with Carrots and Bhutan Red Rice

Makes 4–5 servings

Use any kind of mushrooms you like in this recipe. Dried porcinis have a rich flavor and work great alongside any others. If you can find them inexpensively, add a few dried or fresh morel mushrooms—they are amazingly rich.

2 tablespoons extra virgin olive oil

1 yellow onion

4 carrots, diced

1 cup Bhutan red rice

4 cups vegetable broth

2 cups water

1 ½ cups cooking sherry

¼ ounce dry chanterelle mushrooms, reconstituted

2 ounces fresh king oyster mushrooms, sliced

½ ounce dried porcini mushrooms, reconstituted

8 ounces fresh cremini mushrooms

4 tablespoons Earth Balance®, ghee, or butter

3 cloves garlic, smashed and minced

1 bay leaf

2 tablespoons fresh parsley, minced

1 tablespoon fresh thyme, or about 1½ teaspoons dried

1 teaspoon dry or fresh sage, rubbed

Pink salt and pepper to taste

Option: Add the dry mushrooms to a bowl with a little hot water and microwave for about 2 minutes covered. Then allow to sit on the counter for about 15 minutes to reconstitute. Keep the water aside to use as part of the broth for the soup.

In a large pot, heat a little extra virgin olive oil. Add onions and carrots. Sauté and cook covered for about 4 minutes. Add in all the remaining ingredients and cook over medium heat, stirring occasionally. Cook for about 20 minutes or until the rice is cooked.

If you want the soup to be thicker, once cooked, take about 1 cup of the mixture and blend it in a food processor and add it back into the soup.

Option: for an even richer flavor, add about ¼ cup red wine while cooking the soup.

Spicy Mexican Chicken with Penne and Peppers

Makes a full skillet—about 4 servings

Drizzle of extra virgin olive oil or grapeseed oil

1 small yellow onion, diced

3 large garlic cloves, smashed and
minced

½ green bell pepper, julienne sliced

½ red bell pepper, julienne sliced

½ yellow bell pepper, julienne sliced

½ orange bell pepper, julienne sliced (or
use more peppers if desired)

2 chipotle peppers in adobo, minced
(look for them canned in the grocery
aisle)*

1 teaspoon Mexican oregano, dried or
fresh, rubbed

2–3 tablespoons fresh cilantro, chopped

1 12-ounce can fire-roasted tomatoes in
green chilies, drained (or look for them
in garlic too)

1 cup vegetable broth or chicken broth

8 ounces gluten-free penne pasta

2–3 chicken breast cutlets, sliced to
make 4–6 pieces

Pink salt and cayenne pepper to taste

Garnish with lime, cotija cheese, and
chopped cilantro

*or substitute 1½ teaspoons chipotle
powder

In a skillet over medium-high heat, add a little extra virgin olive oil. Add in onion and garlic and cook for about 5 minutes. Add in peppers and cook further another 5 minutes until tender. Add 1 minced chipotle, oregano, cilantro, tomatoes, and broth. Add salt and pepper to taste. Cook for about 5 minutes, stirring occasionally.

Cook pasta according to package instructions. Then drain.

Add pasta to the skillet of vegetables and stir to combine gently. Then cover and turn off heat while chicken is being cooked.

For the Chicken:
Place chicken in a bowl with a minced chipotle with a little of the adobo seasoning from the can. Add a few shakes of salt. Grill on an interior grill top or an outside grill grate that's been coated with cooking spray. Cook over medium-high heat covered for about 4–5 minutes per side or until internal temperature reaches 165 degrees F. Remove immediately.

Plate pasta and peppers and add chicken on top. Garnish with lime, cotija cheese, and fresh cilantro.

Easy Paella

Makes 4–6 servings (depending on how hungry your guests are)

1 cup clam juice (or more if you want
to use the whole jar)

½ cup chicken or vegetable broth
(or water)

½ cup Bhutan red rice

6 garlic cloves, smashed and minced

½ cup white onion, diced

½ large sweet red bell pepper, sliced into
strips

½ large yellow or orange bell pepper,
sliced into strips

2 pinches of saffron (about ½ teaspoon)

Cayenne pepper

2–3 all natural chicken andouille sausage
links (make sure they are gluten-free)

1 tomato, cored and diced

6–8 large shrimp, shelled, rinsed,
deveined if desired (leave tails on)

1 cup fresh or frozen peas

4–5 fresh clams or mussels, rinsed and
scrubbed

Sea salt or pink salt and fresh cracked
pepper to taste

About ¼ cup water

Fresh flat-leaf parsley

2 lemons, sliced into wedges, seeded

In a large skillet or paella skillet over high heat, add clam juice, broth, and rice. Bring to a boil, then cover and reduce to low. Add garlic and onions and peppers. Stir. Add in saffron and a few shakes of cayenne pepper. Continue to cook until rice is tender.

In a separate skillet, cook andouille sausage links until browned.

Add tomato and cooked sausage to the skillet and stir. Add in raw shrimp and cook about 5 minutes. Add in fresh or frozen peas and the clams or mussels. Add in a few cranks of fresh ground salt. Add in about ¼ cup or ½ cup of water if it's getting too dry.

Paella is done when the shrimp are firm and pink and the clams and/or mussels have opened. Remove skillet from heat and allow to rest about 5 minutes. Toss in parsley and fresh-squeezed lemon. Serve with additional wedges of lemon.

Mexican Black Bean Stack with Vegetables, Red Quinoa, and Brown Rice

Makes 2 servings

Want to impress a guest with a yummy dish? Here's the super fast way to make a lovely-looking low-fat dish with lots of flavor. A biscuit cutter or culinary cylinder will come in handy for this recipe.

2 medium zucchini, sliced to about ⅛-inch thick

1 12-ounce can Muir Glen Organic Diced Fire Roasted Tomatoes with Green Chilies®

Drizzle of olive oil

1 package Seeds of Change Fully Cooked Quinoa and Brown Rice® (or if you can't locate that, use about 3 cups of fully cooked brown rice and 1 cup of cooked red quinoa)

1 12-ounce can organic black beans, drained and rinsed

1 teaspoon taco seasoning or fajita seasoning

For garnish, top with a few sprinkles of cotija cheese, crumbled

A few leaves of cilantro

Preparing the Zucchini:
Coat the sliced zucchini with cooking spray olive oil and cook inside on a cast iron griddle until tender. Or simply cook in a regular skillet until tender, turning once or twice until slightly browned. Once done, set aside.

Preparing the Sauce:
In a food processor, puree the can of tomato and chilies. Transfer to a saucepan and heat through.

The Beans and Rice/Quinoa Stack:
In a skillet over medium heat, add a drizzle of olive oil. Heat the cooked quinoa and brown rice package and black beans. Stir in the taco seasoning. Sprinkle a few crumbs of cotija cheese and stir. Once the ingredients are heated through, about 2–3 minutes, set aside.

Assembly:
Place the cylinder in the middle of the plate. With a serving spoon, take the brown rice/quinoa/black bean mixture and fill the cylinder. Pack it firmly with the back of the spoon until the desired height is reached—about 1½–2 inches high. Then carefully lift up to remove the cylinder. Arrange a few slices of the zucchini on top of the stack. With a spoon, surround the stack with a thin layer of sauce. Sprinkle the cotija cheese over the plate. Garnish with a few cilantro leaves and serve immediately.

NOTE: You'll need a biscuit cutter other round kitchen mold with two open ends.

Shortcuts:
Look for fully cooked grilled zucchini and eggplant in the freezer case. They work great!

NOTE: If you have any leftover beans and rice mixture, use it for an open-faced burrito for lunch later in the week.

Rustic Chicken with Asparagus, Sun-Dried Tomatoes, and Mushrooms

Makes 4–5 servings

2 tablespoons extra virgin olive oil

2–3 large garlic cloves, smashed and minced

2 chicken breasts, boneless and skinless and sliced into thin pieces

Fresh cracked black pepper to taste

About 2½ cups brown rice spiral pasta (or another of your favorite gluten-free pastas)

4–6 cremini mushrooms, sliced (or use porcini mushrooms for richer flavor)

2 cups fresh spinach

¼ cup plain goat cheese (not herbed)

1 cup seasoned fire-roasted tomatoes (look for them on salad bars) or use rehydrated sun-dried tomatoes*

¼ cup Kalamata olives, whole

3–4 stalks asparagus, fully cooked

Red chili flakes and *Optional:* A few pine nuts.

Preparation Tip:
Between 1 and 3 hours before you begin cooking, add the garlic to the olive oil and set on the counter covered. This will release the peppery taste of the garlic into the oil and add an awesome layer of flavor to the recipe.

In a skillet over medium heat, add a drizzle of extra virgin olive oil and cook the chicken, stirring occasionally. While cooking, add in some fresh cracked pepper. Once cooked through, about 5–8 minutes, remove from heat and set aside.

In a pot, heat water to a boil and cook the pasta according to package instructions. Once done, remove from heat, drain in a colander, and set aside.

In the same skillet used for the chicken, drizzle a little of the garlicky olive oil and toss in the mushrooms and cook for about 3 minutes. Then add the spinach. As the spinach heats up, it will reduce in volume. Once that occurs, toss in all the remaining ingredients. The goat cheese will melt slightly and create a nice light sauce. If at this point it seems too dry, add a little more olive oil and serve immediately.

*Some sun-dried tomatoes come in a jar with olive oil and herbs. Those are fine; however, some brands are very high in sodium. You may be better off using a package of dry sun-dried tomatoes and soak them in warm water to rehydrate them before using in the recipe.

Chapter 5: Baking, Muffins, Loaves, and Bars

Cherry Almond Biscotti with Cocoa Nibs

Makes about 12–14 pieces
Preheat oven to 300 degrees F.

½ cup coconut oil, room temperature

¾ cup coconut sugar

3 teaspoons vanilla extract

2 eggs

1¾ cup all-purpose gluten-free baking
   flour

¼ teaspoon pink salt

1 teaspoon baking powder

1 teaspoon cinnamon

½ cup dried tart cherries

½ cup coarsely chopped almonds

3 teaspoons slivered almonds

½ cup cocoa nibs or chocolate chips

In a large bowl, combine coconut oil and coconut sugar until well blended. Add vanilla and eggs and whisk for about a minute.

In a medium bowl, combine flour, salt, baking powder, and cinnamon. Slowly add flour mixture to the wet mixture. Fold in cherries, slivered almonds, and cocoa nib with your hands.

On a parchment-lined baking tray, form a loaf with the dough about 8 inches x 4 inches.

Bake for about 30–35 minutes.

Allow to cool completely before adding chocolate drizzle.

For Chocolate Drizzle:
1 cup semi-sweet chocolate chips

To add a drizzle of chocolate overtop: Melt about 1 cup of semi-sweet chocolate chips in a saucepan, stirring constantly so they don't burn. Once melted, remove from heat and allow to cool slightly. Using a spatula or large spoon, place in a pastry bag with a small frosting hole cap or cut a small corner off of a freezer bag and squeeze chocolate overtop of the biscotti. Using a serrated knife, slice the biscotti into ½-inch thick bars. Place back on baking tray and bake for another 12–15 minutes.

Note: If the dough is sticky, you may wish to grease your hands with butter or cooking spray before mixing it.

Pear Cranberry Crumble

Makes 1 pie pan (about 8–10 servings)
Preheat oven to 350 degrees F.

Filling:

4 large pears, peeled, cored, and sliced
   thin (about 6 cups)

3 tablespoons coconut sugar

1 tablespoon lemon juice

1 teaspoon lemon zest

1 teaspoon vanilla extract

2 teaspoons arrowroot

1 teaspoon ground ginger

1 teaspoon cinnamon

¼ teaspoon nutmeg

¾ cup dried cranberries

2 tablespoons butter, ghee, or Earth
   Balance®

Crumble Topping:

1¾ cup quick-cook oats

1 teaspoon cinnamon

½ teaspoon vanilla extract

Dash of salt

4 tablespoons coconut flour

⅓ cup coconut sugar

1 cup butter, cold (or ½ cup butter and
   ½ cup coconut oil)

Optional: Add a dollop of strained Labneh
   or nonfat vanilla yogurt on top.

Combine all filling ingredients in a medium bowl. Place filling into a buttered/greased pie pan.

Place crumble topping ingredients in a medium bowl and combine using an electric mixer. Do not overmix.

Spread crumble mixture evenly over the filling.

Bake for 20–25 minutes or until top is golden brown.

Serve warm.

Simple Gluten-Free Fruit Tart

Makes 1 9-inch tart
Preheat oven to 350 degrees F.

Ever heard of Labneh? It's a super-delicious strained yogurt that is absolutely decadent! It's also commonly called Lebanese cream cheese. You'll most likely find this in a health food or Middle Eastern grocery store. Watch out though—it is somewhat high in calories since it's so dense!

If you can't locate Labneh, no worries; use any plain nonfat Greek-style yogurt instead—Fage® (pronounced Fah-yay) is the thickest I have discovered.

For this recipe, I used forelle pears, which are small and simply gorgeous with their red speckles and yellow skin. They have a very rich fragrant flavor and are slightly crisp. Look for them when they are in season! Any pear will work in this recipe, but keep the little forelles in mind if you see them.

For the Crust:
1 large egg (from a happy hen that's free-ranged)
2 cups hazelnut flour, (or use 1 cup hazelnut flour and 1 cup almond meal)
1 teaspoon tapioca flour (or more if it seems too crumbly)
½ teaspoon fine pink salt or fine sea salt
2 tablespoons coconut oil, liquid at room temperature or melted
1 tablespoon butter, softened or melted
Plus more coconut oil or coconut oil cooking spray to coat (and more to coat the pan)

For the Creamy Stuff:
About 8 ounces of Labneh strained yogurt (or plain nonfat Greek-style yogurt)
1 teaspoon vanilla extract
½ teaspoon lemon zest

For the Topping:
Any fruits and berries you like! (I used sliced kiwi, blueberries, raspberries, and forelle pears)
About ¼ cup apricot preserves (look for all natural without added sugar)
1–2 tablespoons water

Place the crust ingredients in a food processor and blend them briefly until they form a ball.

With a spatula scrape the sides down and remove the dough. Place it in the center of a 9-inch metal tart pan that's been sprayed with coconut cooking oil or other cooking oil. Spread the dough out, pressing it into the pan with the bottom of a large spoon or your hands. Tamp down the edges to make them even.

Place in middle oven rack and cook for 15–18 minutes or until the edges are slightly browned. All oven temperatures vary slightly so keep an eye on it so it doesn't burn.

While the crust is cooking, in a small bowl stir the Labneh or Greek-style yogurt, vanilla extract, and lemon zest together. Then set aside.

Once the crust is cooked, allow to cool and carefully remove the tart with a spatula and place on a large plate or tray.

Spread the cream mixture evenly on the tart.

Cover the tart with the fruit any way you like without being too fussy.

Add 1–2 tablespoons of water to apricot preserves and mix with a spoon to make it slightly more liquefied. It will have chunks of apricots, which is fine, but add a little more water if necessary to make sure it can be drizzled well. With a spoon, drizzle the preserve "glaze" over the tart.

For serving, carefully cut the pieces into wedges with a sharp knife. The crust may be quite crumbly, so be gentle when picking them up with a spatula.

Easy tip: You can prepare this in a 9-inch pizza pan if you don't have a tart pan. In fact, a pizza pan makes it easier because you can just slide the cooked crust out onto your serving tray.

Blueberry Betty's—Vegan!

Makes 12–14
Preheat oven to 350 degrees F.

I wasn't quite sure what to call these. They originally were going to be scones, but turned out to be more moist than a scone. And they aren't quite a muffin either. So . . . Blueberry Betty's is what I've decided on! Basically they are a cross between a drop cookie and a muffin. And really all you need to know is—they are worth trying!

1 cup almond meal

½ cup coconut flour

½ cup tapioca starch

1 teaspoon pink salt

¾ cup xanthan gum

1 teaspoon baking soda

2 teaspoons baking powder

1½ teaspoons cinnamon

4 tablespoons coconut oil
   (room temperature)

1½ teaspoons vanilla extract

¾ cup applesauce

3 tablespoons honey
   (or blue agave nectar)

⅓ cup plus 3 tablespoons almond milk,
   unsweetened

¾ to 1 cup fresh blueberries, if available
   (if not use frozen, slightly thawed)

1 tablespoon coconut sugar

In a medium bowl, combine almond meal, coconut flour, tapioca starch, salt, xanthan gum, baking soda, baking powder, and cinnamon.

In a small bowl, combine all wet ingredients except blueberries and stir together.

Add wet mixture to dry mixture and stir to combine. Fold in blueberries gently.

Drop dough (about 2 tablespoons of batter) onto parchment paper–lined cookie sheet.

Sprinkle with a little coconut sugar and a little extra cinnamon if desired.

Bake 20–25 minutes.

Raspberry Oatmeal Bars with Chia, Pepita, and Flax Seeds

Makes about 18 bars
Preheat oven to 350 degrees F.

1 cup teff flour

¾ cup amaranth flour (plus 1 tablespoon reserved)

1 cup coconut sugar

¼ teaspoon pink salt

½ teaspoon baking soda

1 tablespoon flax seed (brown or golden)

2 tablespoons chia seeds

1 cup butter (softened and cut into pieces)

1½ cups oats

Zest of 2 oranges (about 1½ teaspoons)

4 teaspoons pepita seeds

7 tablespoons raspberry preserves (low sugar preferred)

In a medium bowl, combine teff flour, amaranth flour, coconut sugar, salt, baking soda, flax seeds, chia seeds, and butter.

Combine until crumbly dough forms. Add in oats and orange zest and mix until well combined.

Coat a 9 x 13 glass pan with cooking spray. Coat pan with about a tablespoon of amaranth flour. Discard any extra that may be loose in the pan.

Press half to two-thirds of the dough into the bottom of the pan using your hands. Top with raspberry preserves. Press remaining dough on top and gently press down. Top with pepita seeds.

Bake 35–40 minutes. Cool completely before cutting into bars.

Pineapple Coconut Muffins

Dense and delicious little buggers!

Makes 12 large muffins or about 2 dozen regular size
Preheat oven to 350 degrees F.

4¾ cups almond flour or almond meal

½ tablespoon baking powder

½ teaspoon baking soda

2½ tablespoons cinnamon

½ teaspoon ginger, ground (or use fresh
    grated for extra peppery taste)

½ teaspoon nutmeg, ground

2 cups crushed canned pineapple
    (retain the juice)

½ cup honey

¾ cup coconut sugar

¼ cup coconut oil, room temperature

3 teaspoons vanilla extract

½ cup pineapple juice (from the can)

1½ cups walnuts or macadamia nuts,
    chopped

3 eggs, lightly beaten

1 cup unsweetened coconut, either
    shredded or flaked plus a little extra
    for topping

1 cup carrot, grated (about 1 large carrot)

Zest and juice of 1 large orange
    (about ½ cup of juice)

½ cup evaporated fat-free milk or almond
    milk, unsweetened

In a large bowl, combine all ingredients until well mixed using a spoon. Spray an oversized muffin tin with cooking or baking spray and dust with a little almond meal or other gluten-free flour.

Fill each muffin hole about two-thirds full.

Top each muffin with a little extra shredded or flaked coconut (about ½ teaspoon each).

Bake 45–50 minutes or until an inserted toothpick comes out clean.

Spicy Brownies

Makes about 15 2-inch square brownies

2 cups Bob's Red Mill Gluten-free Baking Powder®

¾ cup unsweetened cocoa powder

1 teaspoon baking powder

2 teaspoons cinnamon, ground

1 teaspoon cardamom, ground

1 teaspoon sea salt plus extra to top brownies

1 teaspoon guajillo pepper, ground (or another medium-hot chili powder)

¼ cup coconut oil, room temperature, or slightly more

½ cup butter or ghee, melted

1 tablespoon vanilla extract

⅓ cup water or almond milk

In a large bowl, combine all dry ingredients.

In a medium bowl, combine all wet ingredients and whisk until well blended.

Add wet mixture to dry and whisk until combined.

Coat a 8 x 11.5 glass baking pan with cooking spray.

Bake for 45–50 minutes. Sprinkle a little extra pink salt or sea salt on top.

Cool for at least 10 minutes before cutting into squares.

Gluten-Free Banana Bread with Macadamia Nuts

Makes one 9 x 5–inch loaf pan
Preheat oven to 350 degrees F.

What's not to like about bananas, macadamia nuts, and cocoa nibs? Not a darn thing! Use this as a base and make endless variations with a wide variety of nuts!

1 teaspoon vanilla

1 cup coconut sugar

4 tablespoons coconut oil, room temperature

6 tablespoons almond milk, unsweetened (or milk)

2 eggs, lightly beaten

3 ripe bananas, mashed (can be previously frozen, thawed also)

1 cup hazelnut flour

1 cup sorghum flour

1 teaspoon baking soda

½ to ¾ teaspoon cinnamon

⅔ cup or slightly more macadamia nuts, chopped loosely

½ cup cocoa nibs, or semi-sweet chocolate chips

In a medium bowl, combine vanilla, coconut sugar, coconut oil, almond milk, eggs, and bananas. Stir well until combined.

In a large bowl, combine hazelnut flour, sorghum flour, baking soda, cinnamon, macadamia nuts, and cocoa nibs.

Add flour mixture to wet mixture and stir just until combined.

Spray loaf pan with cooking spray and dust with a little sorghum flour. Discard excess flour. Pour batter in and bake for 55–60 minutes or until an inserted wooden skewer or knife comes out clean.

Savory Corn and Cheese Muffins

Makes about 1 dozen
Preheat oven to 350 degrees F.

2 to 3 teaspoons shallots, chopped

½ cup red bell pepper, seeded and
chopped

1 cup corn meal (corn flour)

1 cup quinoa flour (or sorghum flour)

1 tablespoon baking powder

1½ teaspoons pink salt or sea salt

1 teaspoon cayenne pepper

1½ teaspoons paprika (or 1 teaspoon
Hungarian hot paprika)

1 large egg, lightly beaten

1 cup plus 1 tablespoon almond milk,
unsweetened

⅓ cup coconut oil

1½ cup fresh baby spinach, chopped
roughly

3 tablespoons fresh basil leaves,
chopped

1 cup manchego cheese (or ½ cup
parmesan or pecorino romano cheese
and ½ cup cheddar—half cup for the
batter and half for muffin tops)

In a small skillet over medium heat, sauté shallots and red pepper for about 4 minutes or until tender.

In a medium bowl, combine all other ingredients, reserving ½ cup of cheese for the tops of muffins.

Add in shallots and red pepper. Combine mixture with spoon.

Fill lightly greased muffin tin or lined muffin tin about two-thirds full of batter. Top with a little extra cheese and bake for about 12–15 minutes or until an inserted toothpick comes out clean.

Cool completely before serving.

Lemon Poppy Seed Corn Muffins

Use mini muffin tins with paper liners for this recipe.

Makes about 3 dozen mini muffins
Preheat oven to 375 degrees F.

1½ cups almond meal/flour

¾ cup yellow corn meal

⅔ cup coconut sugar

1 tablespoon baking powder

½ teaspoon pink salt or sea salt

1 tablespoon poppy seeds

¼ cup almond milk, unsweetened, or any
   kind of milk

2 large eggs, lightly beaten

⅓ cup melted butter or ghee

3 tablespoons coconut oil, room
   temperature

Juice and zest of 2 lemons (about ½ cup)

Combine dry ingredients in a large bowl and stir until blended.

In a medium bowl, combine all wet ingredients and stir until well blended.

Add wet mixture to dry mixture and stir to combine well.

Pour batter into paper-lined mini muffin tins about two-thirds full.

Bake about 10 minutes or until an inserted toothpick comes out clean.

Ginger Cardamom Bars

Makes one 9 x 5–inch loaf pan about 2 inches high
Preheat oven to 350 degrees F.

2 cups almond flour

½ teaspoon pink salt or sea salt

3 teaspoons cardamom, ground

1 cup coconut sugar

½ cup coconut oil, room temperature
  (or melted butter)

½ cup maple syrup or blue agave nectar

3 large eggs, room temperature

1 teaspoon apple cider vinegar

1 teaspoon almond extract

1 cup crystalized ginger chips/pieces

Optional: slivered almonds for the tops of
  the bars

Spray loaf pan lightly with cooking spray.

In a large bowl, add almond flour, pink salt, cardamom, and coconut sugar, and make a little well in the center of the ingredients.

In a large bowl, combine coconut oil, maple syrup, eggs, vinegar, and almond extract. Slowly add the wet ingredients into the well of the dry ingredients. Stir to combine. Fold in ginger chips.

Pour into prepared pan and bake for about 45–50 minutes or until an inserted toothpick comes out clean.

Allow to cool for about an hour before adding frosting. Once frosted, cut into ½-inch bars. Store in refrigerator with parchment paper or wax paper in between layers if you are stacking them in an airtight container.

Gooey Chocolate Espresso Brownies

Adapted from my friend Kelli Felix's amazing recipe!

Makes about 15 2-inch square brownies

2 cups Bob's Red Mill Gluten-Free 1 to 1
   Baking Flour®
¾ cup unsweetened dark cocoa powder
   (or regular baking cocoa powder)
1 teaspoon baking powder
1 teaspoon sea salt plus extra to top
   brownies
2–4 teaspoons instant espresso
1¾ cups sugar
1½ cups plus 3 teaspoons coffee
   (previously brewed and cold or room
   temperature)
1 cup vegetable oil (or ½ cup coconut oil
   and ½ cup avocado, smashed)
½ cup butter or ghee, melted
2 teaspoons vanilla extract

In a large bowl, combine all dry ingredients.

In a medium bowl, combine all wet ingredients and whisk until well blended.

Add wet mixture to dry and whisk until combined.

Spray an 8 x 11.5 glass baking pan with cooking spray. Bake for 45–50 minutes. Sprinkle a little extra pink salt or sea salt on top.

Cool for at least 10 minutes before cutting into squares.

Date Nut Cookies

Simply put, these are the bomb! For a different twist, add in goji berries or other types of nuts.

Makes about 26 2-inch cookies
Preheat oven to 375 degrees F.

1 egg, beaten

1 teaspoon vanilla extract

2 tablespoons Earth Balance® or butter,
    softened

1 cup quick-cook oats

½ cup almond meal/flour

⅛ cup Bob's Gluten-Free baking mix®

½ cup tapioca flour

½ cup coconut sugar

1 teaspoon baking powder

⅛ teaspoon pink salt or sea salt

1 cup Medjool dates, pitted, chopped
    (or any kind of date pieces)

Optional: ½ cup slivered almonds

Line a baking tray with parchment paper or grease a baking tray with cooking spray.

In a medium bowl combine egg, vanilla, and Earth Balance® and stir until blended.

Add dry ingredients except for dates. Mix with a spoon until blended.

Add wet ingredients to dry and stir until mixed well. Add in date pieces and stir.

Spoon about ½ tablespoon amounts of batter onto prepared baking sheet.

Bake 7–9 minutes or until edges of cookies become golden brown.

Cool a few minutes before removing from baking tray.

Store in a container with layers of parchment paper or wax paper in between stacks of cookies so they don't stick.

Coconut Lemon Cake

Makes 1 9-inch cake or about 8 small mini-loaf cakes
Preheat oven to 350 degrees F.

For the Cake:

1 teaspoon cream of tartar

4 large eggs, separated (but keep both
   the yolks and the whites)

¾ teaspoon baking powder

¼ cup coconut flour, sifted

Pinch of pink salt

3 tablespoons honey

4 tablespoons coconut oil, room
   temperature

1½ teaspoons vanilla extract

4 tablespoons freshly grated lemon zest

4 teaspoons fresh lemon juice

½ cup coconut sugar

Parchment paper

Coat cake tins with cooking spray (I used coconut cooking spray). Then line the bottom with parchment paper.

In a large bowl add cream of tartar and egg whites. Whip until stiff peaks form.

Mix in baking powder, flour, coconut sugar, and salt.

Place egg yolks, honey, coconut oil, vanilla extract, lemon zest, and lemon juice in a medium bowl. Stir together. Sift in baking powder and flour combination into the egg yolk mixture until fully blended

Fold about a cup of the egg whites into the mixture to lighten. Then add in the remaining egg whites, keeping them as light and airy as possible.

Pour batter into cake pans about two-thirds full. Bake for about 18–20 minutes or until an inserted toothpick comes out clean. Note: make sure not to overbake these pups!

Allow to cool on wire cooling racks a few minutes. Then flip them over on the rack and remove the parchment to finish cooling the cakes.

Spread frosting overtop only after the cakes are completely cooled. Store in refrigerator once frosted.

For the Frosting:

¼ cup coconut oil

1 teaspoon agave nectar or honey

1 teaspoon lemon juice, fresh

1½ tablespoons lemon zest, fresh

Dash of pink salt

½ cup goat cheese

1 cup unsweetened coconut flakes
   (or shredded coconut)

Whisk all ingredients together except for coconut flakes until frosting is fluffy. Spread on cooled cakes with a spatula. Sprinkle the coconut flakes on top. Store frosted cake in refrigerator.

Note: Frosting will firm back up in the refrigerator.

Pumpkin Bars with Cocoa Nibs and Goat Cheese Frosting

Makes about 20–24 bars
Preheat oven to 350 degrees F.

1½ cups all-purpose gluten-free flour
   (I used Bob's Red Mill®)

½ cup hazelnut flour

1 teaspoon baking soda

4 teaspoons cinnamon

2½ teaspoons allspice

½ teaspoon nutmeg

1 teaspoon pink salt

4 eggs

1½ cups coconut sugar

⅔ cup agave nectar

3 tablespoons coconut oil

½ cup applesauce

1 15.5-ounce can pumpkin

4 teaspoons vanilla

4 tablespoons butter, melted

Dash of salt

3 tablespoons cocoa nibs,
   or chocolate chips

In a small bowl, whisk flours, baking soda, cinnamon, allspice, nutmeg, and salt.

In a large bowl, beat eggs, coconut sugar, agave nectar, coconut oil, applesauce, pumpkin, butter, and vanilla with an electric mixer until well combined.

Add in flour mixture and mix until just combined.

Coat an 11 x 15 glass pan with cooking spray. Pour mixture in and smooth the top with a spatula. Bake 30–35 minutes. Allow to cool completely—at least an hour.

Coat with frosting and cut into squares or bars. Keep in refrigerator.

Goat Cheese Frosting:

12 ounces plain goat cheese

½ cup butter or Earth Balance™, softened

½ cup coconut oil, room temperature

½ cup agave nectar

2 teaspoons vanilla extract

In a large bowl, combine all ingredients with an electric mixer. To thicken frosting, place in refrigerator before topping the bars. Store frosted bars in a sealed container in the refrigerator.

Chocolate Bundt Cake with Guajillo Pepper and Spicy Sweet Frosting

Use a bundt pan for this recipe.

Preheat oven to 350 degrees F.

For the Cake:

1 cup amaranth flour

1 cup coconut flour

1 cup coconut sugar

4 tablespoons cocoa powder

2 teaspoons cinnamon

½ teaspoon xanthan gum

1 teaspoon baking soda

2 teaspoons baking powder

½ cup tapioca starch

Pinch of pink salt

½ cup coconut oil

2 large eggs, whisked

1 teaspoon vanilla

½ cup cocoa nibs or semi-sweet
   chocolate chips

1 cup dried tart cherries

In large bowl, whisk all dry ingredients together except for cocoa nibs and dried cherries.

Add coconut oil, eggs, and vanilla extract. Whisk until smooth. Fold in cocoa nibs and dried cherries. Pour batter into bundt pan coated with cooking spray.

Bake for about an hour or until a wooden skewer or knife inserted comes out clean. Allow the cake to cool for 5 minutes before turning it over on a wire rack to remove it. Once it's cool, place the wire rack on top of the bundt cake pan; flip it over and lift off the pan. Allow to cool further before adding glaze.

Before glazing cake, you may wish to transfer the cake to a serving tray.

Drizzle spicy sweet glaze over top portions of the cake and allow to drizzle down the sides.

For the Spicy Sweet Frosting:

1 cup nonfat vanilla yogurt

1 cup goat cheese

1 teaspoon vanilla

2 teaspoons honey or agave nectar

½ teaspoon guajillo pepper powder (or any kind of
   medium-hot chili powder)

Place ingredients in a small bowl and mix together. Generously pour over cake and allow to drizzle over the edges. Store in refrigerator to thicken frosting before cutting and serving.

Store cake in the refrigerator.

PARTY TO DO

1. HEAT UP APPETIZERS
2. SET TABLE
3. PLACEMATS
4. CHILL WHITE WINE
5. MAKE SAUCE FOR SHRIMP
6. VACCUM

Chapter 6: Small Bites
Hors d'oeuvres for Small Parties

Zucchini Roll-Up Appetizers with Smoked Paprika Hummus

Makes about 5 roll-ups for each medium zucchini

For this recipe you can use an outside grill, an inside electric grill, grill top, or even just cook the zucchini in a skillet. Either way, cook the slices of zucchini until they are just tender and not too soft.

3–4 zucchini, sliced ¼ inch thick
   (with skins on)
Olive oil or cooking spray
1 small container store-bought hummus,
   plain or garlic
1 teaspoon fresh squeezed lemon juice
About a teaspoon smoked paprika
5 fire-roasted or sun-dried tomatoes
   (the kind found on salad bars or in jars
   with olive oil)
Toothpicks

Outdoor Grill Method:
Preheat gas grill on high with lid closed, or if using charcoal grill, prepare for direct heat cooking over hot charcoal. If you are using a gas grill, reduce the temperature of the grill to medium-high. Carefully coat the grill surface with cooking spray, spraying at an angle.

While the grill is heating up, carefully slice zucchini lengthwise into ¼-inch strips.

Brush olive oil or spray cooking oil on zucchini strips. Place directly on grill to cook about 4 minutes, turning once. When they are slightly tender, remove from grill to cool.

Inside Grill Top or Electric George Foreman–Style Method:
Heat grill to high heat. Coat the grill surface with cooking spray.

Place the zucchini strips directly on the grill and cook until tender. Cooking times may vary depending on if you have a lid or not. Cook until tender but not too soft.

In a medium-sized bowl, add hummus, lemon juice, and smoked paprika and stir together.

Once cooled, add about 1½ tablespoons hummus to the edge of a zucchini strip and roll up. Place a toothpick through the hummus to keep zucchini together. Place directly on serving tray. Garnish each roll-up with a slice or two of fire-roasted tomatoes. Roll-ups can be served chilled or at room temperature.

Stuffed Sunburst (Pattypan) Squash, Red Curry Shrimp, and Kañiwa

Makes 6 servings
Preheat oven to 400 degrees F.

Look for sunburst or Pattypan squash in season. If they aren't available, you can substitute yellow squash cut in half lengthwise instead. Simply scoop out a little of the yellow squash first prior to stuffing.

½ cup kañiwa

1 cup vegetable broth or water

1 garlic clove, smashed, minced

Pink salt to taste

2 teaspoons onion, chopped fine

6 sunburst "pattypans"

2 teaspoons Thai red curry paste

¼ to ½ cup light canned coconut milk

8–10 medium fully cooked shrimp, cut into bite-sized pieces

About 4 teaspoons fresh cilantro, chopped

Juice of 2 limes

Cook the kañiwa in 1 cup water or vegetable broth in a small saucepan over high heat. Add the garlic, a pinch of salt, and onion. Bring to a boil and then cover and reduce to low. Simmer for about 15 minutes or until the water has evaporated. Turn off heat and allow to sit for 5–7 minutes. The grains will sprout and you know they are done when you see a little white thread coming out of the grain.

Cut the tops off the squash about ½ inch from the top, depending on the size of squash you have. Scoop out the insides of the squash and set aside in a medium bowl.

Place the squash and the tops on a baking tray lined with tinfoil or parchment paper. Bake for about 10 minutes or until soft, but not fully cooked.

In a skillet, add the red curry paste and coconut milk. Cook on medium heat and whisk ingredients together. Add the cooked shrimp and cilantro and a few dashes of salt. Then set aside.

Once the rice is cooked, toss it into the skillet and stir to coat.

Once the squash is done, stuff the squash with the kañiwa and shrimp mixture.

Bake on a baking sheet for about 15 minutes or until the squash is tender. Remove from oven and squirt fresh lime juice into the cup and add the top onto squash.

Serve the squash with a wedge of lime and garnish plate with a little chopped red pepper and/or fresh cilantro. Or decorate the plate with dots or zigzags of sriracha sauce around the plate.

Hot Smoked Salmon Crostini with Hummus, Dill, and Capers

Makes 8–10 or more
Preheat oven to 400 degrees F.

How you assemble the ingredients in this recipe is up to you, so the measurements are approximate.

4–5 pieces whole-grain gluten-free bread

Extra virgin olive oil or cooking spray

Pink salt and fresh cracked pepper

Fresh lemon (optional)

About ¼ cup fresh dill, chopped

1½ teaspoons hummus per piece of
  bread

¼ teaspoon of capers per crostini

About 3 ounces of hot smoked salmon

Dash of hot paprika or smoked paprika
  for each crostini

Cut the crusts off the gluten-free bread slices and feed the crust to the birds or discard. Cut the slices into quarters. Brush each piece with a little olive oil and add a little salt. Place on a baking sheet and bake until golden brown, about 4–5 minutes per side.

In a small bowl, mix a little fresh lemon juice and a few teaspoons of the dill to your favorite store-bought hummus.

Spread about 1½ teaspoons of hummus to each crostini toast. Sprinkle a few capers on each piece. Add a few crumbles of hot smoked salmon to each piece. Garnish with fresh dill. Add fresh cracked pepper and paprika and serve.

Other options: You can also mix the capers in with the hummus if desired. Use hot smoked white fish instead of hot smoked salmon—or use both!

Red Yams with Black Rice and Goat Cheese

Makes about 8–10 pieces
Preheat oven to 400 degrees F.

1 cup vegetable broth or water
½ cup black rice (also called Forbidden Rice or mahogany rice)
2 large red yams, scrubbed with skins on and sliced into ½- to ¾-inch thick discs
Tofurkey® Vegetarian Chorizo Crumbles, or your favorite all natural sausage
Crumbled goat cheese (about ½ cup)

Optional: garnish with fresh diced cilantro or flat-leaf parsley

In a saucepan over high heat, bring vegetable broth to a boil. Rinse black rice in cold water and drain. Add rice to boiling water, cover, and reduce heat to simmer for about 20–25 minutes or until tender. Once done, set aside.

Place the yams on a baking tray and coat with extra virgin olive oil or cooking spray. Cook for about 20 minutes or until tender.

In a small saucepan or microwave, heat the chorizo crumbles through.

Once the yams are fully cooked, remove from oven and allow to cool slightly before continuing.

Place a spoonful in the center of each slice of yam. Top with the chorizo crumbles and goat cheese. Garnish with fresh herbs and serve immediately.

Grilled Pork Tenderloin Crostini with Mango Chutney

Makes 10–12 pieces, depending on the size of tenderloin
Marinate the pork tenderloin at least 4 hours or overnight for most flavor.

You can grill the pork on your outside grill or use an inside grill grate if you want the nice char marks. If you don't have either one, simply bake on a baking sheet in the oven at 350 degrees F for about 20 minutes. If you have a digital cooking thermometer, it will help you with this recipe so you don't overcook the meat.

3 tablespoons garam masala

2 cloves garlic, smashed and minced

3 teaspoons apple cider vinegar

4 teaspoons extra virgin olive oil

1 pound (give or take) plain pork tenderloin
    cut into ¾- to 1-inch thick medallions

A few dashes of pink salt

1 jar of Major Grey's Hot Mango
    Chutney®

6 pieces gluten-free bread cut into bite-
    sized pieces, crust removed

Fresh diced cilantro and/or finely diced
    red bell pepper for garnish

For the Marinade:
In a medium bowl add garam masala, garlic, apple cider vinegar, olive oil, and salt. Mix thoroughly. Add the pork medallions. Cover and place in refrigerator to marinate at least 4 hours or overnight for even more flavor.

Prior to grilling, allow pork medallions to get to room temperature while the grill heats up. If you are grilling outside, preheat grill on high with lid closed. Once hot, carefully add cooking spray to the surface of the grill grate, or brush on cooking oil. Place pork medallions directly on the grill grate and cook for about 3–4 minutes per side or until the internal temperature of the meat reaches 140 degrees F.

If you are cooking them on a grill grate on the stovetop, add cooking spray to the grill. Place medallions on grill and cook about 4–5 minutes per side or until the internal temperature of the meat reaches 140 degrees F.

Once cooked, place a pork medallion on each piece of bread. Top with about ½ to ¾ teaspoon of chutney and garnish tray with a sprinkling of fresh diced cilantro or finely diced red bell pepper; serve immediately.

Polenta with Turkey, Harissa, and Feta Cheese

Makes 8–10 servings

For the Polenta:

6 cups water

2 cups polenta Bob's Red Mill®
    Polenta Mix

3 tablespoons butter

1 teaspoon chipotle powder

1 teaspoon garlic powder

1½ teaspoons pink salt or sea salt

Extra virgin olive oil or vegetable oil

Toothpicks

For the Toppings:

1 small jar harissa (about 8 ounces)

5–6 slices all natural turkey lunch meat
    (I like Applegate Farms®)

About ¾ cup crumbled feta cheese or
    cotija cheese

Garnish with fresh cilantro and a dusting
    of chipotle powder

In a large, deep pan bring water and salt to a boil over high heat. Slowly add in polenta, stirring frequently. Reduce heat and simmer, stirring frequently to prevent sticking—about 30 minutes. Make sure to use a long handled spoon to stir as the mixture will bubble up and can burn your hand. Add in butter, chipotle powder, garlic powder, and salt and continue stirring a minute more.

Oil a deep medium-sized bowl and lightly coat interior with cooking spray. Spoon polenta mixture into the bowl and allow to stand for about 10 minutes. Once firm, invert onto a flat plate.

It's ready to eat now if you wish to cut it into wedges and top with toppings. Or if you'd like to grill it and add nice grill marks, cut polenta into squares or rectangles and add on top of preheated grill that's been coated with cooking spray. Cook covered for about 3–5 minutes per side until nice grill marks occur. If you don't have a grill, no worries; just cut them into the squares and proceed to the next step.

Allow to cool slightly for better handling. Spread a little harissa on each piece of polenta. Cut the turkey meat into bite-sized pieces and roll up on top of the polenta and stick a toothpick through it. Sprinkle a crumbled feta or cotija cheese and fresh cilantro if desired.

Flatbread Bites with Manchego, Asian Pear, Prosciutto, and Balsamic Glaze

Makes about 5 pieces per tortilla
This recipe is written for 10 pieces of bites
These can be eaten at room temperature and can be made ahead of time.
Preheat oven to 375 degrees F.

2–3 gluten-free tortilla wraps, cut into bite-sized pieces (I love the Gluten-free Pedals®)

2 Asian pears if in season. If not, use any kind of pears such as forelle.*

About ¼ cup manchego cheese, sliced thin with a cheese knife, or grated

About 4 pieces of prosciutto cut into strips

Balsamic glaze (not balsamic vinegar)

On a baking sheet, place the gluten-free tortillas on the tray and bake for about 7–10 minutes or until crispy and firm.

Core and slice the Asian pears and cut into thin pieces. Skins can be left on.

Once the tortilla wraps are done, place on serving tray. Top with pieces of the pears, manchego cheese, and a few strips of the prosciutto. Drizzle the entire area including the tray, with the balsamic glaze in a zigzag decorative formation.

Serve immediately.

* If you are using forelle pears, get about 5 pears since they are smaller than regular pears.

Pistachio-Encrusted Shrimp with Black Mahogany Rice

Makes 8–10
Preheat oven to 400 degrees F.

I use the dressing as a dipping sauce when I'm serving the shrimp on their own. You can add it to the rice for extra flavor or put it in a ramekin on the plate with the rice and shrimp. Take your pick!

1 cup black mahogany rice (I like Lotus Foods Forbidden Rice®)

A few sprigs of fresh cilantro, rough cut

2 ataulfo mangoes, skinned and diced (if not in season, look for regular ripe mangoes)

Pink salt to taste

1 cup pistachios, roasted, salted, and ground

10 large shrimp, raw, shells removed and deveined; tails can be removed if desired

About 1½ egg whites, whisked with an ice cube

For the Dressing (or use as a dipping sauce):

1 cup seasoned rice vinegar

5 tablespoons coconut sugar

At least 1 tablespoon red chili flakes or diced fresh red fresno pepper, or red jalapeño, seeded and minced

For the Rice:
Bring rice and 1¾ cups water to a boil in a large saucepan. Season lightly with salt. Cover, reduce heat to low, and simmer until all liquid is absorbed and rice is tender, about 25 minutes. Remove pan from heat and let stand, covered, for 15 minutes or so.

Once slightly cooled, place in a medium-sized bowl cilantro, 4 tablespoons of the dressing, and mango chunks. Season lightly with pink salt.

For the Shrimp:
In a food processor, grind pistachios and place on a plate. Once shrimp are deveined and shells removed, rinse and pat dry thoroughly with paper towel.

Whisk egg whites. Take a shrimp and dip it into the egg whites. Take your other hand and sprinkle the shrimp with the ground pistachio (rather than dipping into the pistachio). Place on a baking tray lined with parchment paper if you have it. If not, coat baking tray with cooking spray. Once all the shrimp are covered with pistachio, place in oven. Cook for about 7 minutes or until firm and opaque.

For the Dressing (or dipping sauce):
Warm rice vinegar in small saucepan over medium heat. Add coconut sugar and stir until dissolved. Add red chili flakes.

Plating the Dish:
Place about ¼ cup of rice on each plate. Top with a shrimp. Drizzle some of the dressing over the top of the shrimp and rice. Garnish with minced red or yellow pepper or chopped cilantro.

Quick Stuffed Mushrooms with Quinoa and Brown Rice, Dates, and Goat Cheese

Makes 12–15 mushroom caps
Preheat oven to 400 degrees F.

Did you hear that your girlfriend is on her way over with a bottle of wine? Well, you can make this one in a jiffy! No chopping required!

About ½ cup date pieces or dates, pitted and chopped

3 ounces herbed goat cheese

1 8.5 ounce package fully cooked quinoa and brown rice with garlic (Seeds of Change®)*

12–15 cremini mushroom caps (about 1½ inches in width)

Dash or two cayenne pepper or fresh cracked pepper

Optional: garnish with fresh chopped chives or flat-leaf parsley

In a medium bowl, combine dates and herbed goat cheese. Add in fully cooked grains and mix thoroughly.

Pop out the stem of the mushroom cap and discard. With a spoon, take the grain and cheese mixture and pack onto the mushroom cap where the stem was.

Place mushrooms, stuffing side up, on a parchment paper–lined baking tray. Bake for about 15 minutes or so. Transfer to serving tray. If desired, sprinkle fresh chopped herbs over tray. Add dash of cayenne or fresh cracked pepper on top. Serve immediately.

* If you can't find this fully cooked product, look in your grocery aisle for other fully cooked gluten-free rices and quinoas. There's a lot available now in markets! Or simply cook any gluten-free grain you wish to use—about 2 cups when cooked.

Curried Kabocha Smash Toasts

Makes about 10
Preheat oven to 450 degrees F.

1 2½- to 3-pound kabocha, seeded and
    cut into pieces ⅛ to ¼-inch thick

¼ cup extra virgin olive oil

Fresh cracked pepper

½ teaspoon red chili flakes

5 slices gluten-free whole-grain bread,
    cut in half

Pink salt or sea salt

Garam masala or hot curry powder

5 grape or cherry tomatoes, sliced in half

Fresh flat-leaf parsley or cilantro,
    chopped

Carefully slice squash in half by first piercing the skin of it with a sharp knife. Cut all the way through and cut into four pieces. Scoop out seeds and fibers with a spoon and discard. Place pieces in a medium-sized bowl and coat with olive oil. Add fresh cracked pepper and red chili flakes.

Place squash on a parchment paper–lined baking sheet. Spread out flat.

Bake about 15–18 minutes.

While kabocha squash is cooking, coat the bread with a little remaining olive oil. Add salt and pepper.

Place on a baking sheet and bake until golden brown, about 4–5 minutes per side.

When the squash is done, remove and place in a bowl and smash lightly.

Place a dollop of squash on each toast. Sprinkle with garam masala and top with a tomato slice. Garnish tray with fresh herbs if desired.

Chapter 7: Sourcing Guide

The food industry has been following the trends of gluten-free and now offers a wide variety of products available for home cooking as well as some prepared gluten-free foods.

Here is a short list of some mentioned in this book and a few others.

Website Stores:
www.glutenfreemall.com
www.frontiercoop.com
www.seedsofchangefoods.com

Specialty Heirloom Rice:
www.heirloomrice.com
www.lotusfoods.com
www.lundberg.com

Gluten-free Flour:
All Purpose Gluten-free Flour Mix
Almond Meal/ Almond Flour
Amaranth Flour
Buckwheat Flour
Black Bean Flour
Brown Rice Flour
Blue Corn Flour
Corn Flour
Coconut Flour
Flaxseed Meal
Garbanzo Bean Flour
Hazelnut Flour
Oat Flour (non-cross-contaminated)
Mesquite Flour
Millet Flour
Potato Flour
Purple Corn Flour

Purple Yam Flour
Quinoa Flour
Teff Flour
Sorghum Flour
Sprouted Amaranth Flour
Sprouted Black Bean Flour
Sprouted Blue Corn Flour
Sprouted Brown Rice Flour
Sprouted Garbanzo Bean Flour
Sprouted Green Lentil Flour
Sprouted Millet Flour
Sprouted Quinoa Flour
Sprouted Sorghum Flour
Sprouted Teff Flour
Tapioca Flour

Gluten-free Grains:
Uncooked
Amaranth
Bhutan Red Rice
Black Pearl Rice
Black Japonica Rice
Brown Mekong Flower Rice
Buckwheat
Brown Rice
Carnaroli Rice
Heirloom Forbidden Rice
Ifugao Diket Sticky Rice
Jade Pearl Rice

Jasmine Rice
Job's Tears (Hato Mugi)
Kalinga Unoy Heirloom Rice
Kañewa
Oats (non-cross-contaminated)
Madagascar Pink Rice
Mahogany Rice
Mountain Violet Sticky Rice
Mekong Flower Rice
Montina (Indian rice grass)
Millet
Quinoa
Teff
Sorghum
Sprouted Brown Rice
Sprouted Brown Jasmine Rice
Sprouted Red Rice
Tinawon Heirloom Rice
Toasted Buckwheat
Ulikan Red Heirloom Rice
Volcano Rice
Wehani® Rice
Wild Rice

Brands That Offer Fully Cooked Packaged Grains:

Cocomama® Quinoa Cereal—seasoned
Lotus® Rice
Gojo® Rice Bowls
Roland Foods®
Seeds of Change®
Suzi's® Tex Mex Quinoa
Trader Joe's® Fully Wild Rice
Trader Joe's® Fully Cooked Brown Rice—grocery
   aisle and in freezer case
Trader Joe's® Wild and Basmati Rice Pilaf—seasoned
Village Harvest® Fully Cooked Quinoa

Gluten-free Breads:

Some stores have special gluten-free sections of breads and other foods. Also look for some of these breads in the freezer case. Check with a store clerk to show you where the gluten-free products are—they may be hard to find.

Loaves:
Food For Life® Wheat and Gluten-Free Bread (Brown Rice Bread)
Glutino® Flax Seed Bread
Kinnikinnick Gluten-free Bread
Trader Joe's® Gluten-Free Whole Grain Loaf
Udi's® Gluten-Free Foods Whole Grain Bread (look for it in the freezer case)

Flatbreads and Tortilla Wraps:
Sandwich Petals® (my personal favorite!)—3 flavors available: Spinach,
    Garlic, and Pesto
Agave Grain®
Chimayo® Red Chili
Food For Life® Gluten-Free Black Rice Tortilla (look for it in the freezer case)
Glutenfreeda Foods

Sun-dried Tomato and Herbs Tortilla Wraps
Rudi's® Gluten Free Bakery Tortillas—Regular and Spinach (look for it in the
    freezer case)
Sonoma Organic Yellow Corn Tortillas
Udi's® Gluten Free Tortillas (look for it freezer case)

Gluten-free Pastas (dried packaged):
Ancient Harvest®—Black Bean and Quinoa Elbows
Green Lentil & Quinoa Pasta Penne
Bean and Lentil Supergrain Pasta
Quinoa Pasta
Red Lentil and Quinoa Rotelle Pasta
Andean Dream® Quinoa Pastas (Rated Best Gluten-free Pasta by
    Bon Appétit Magazine, 2014)—Spaghetti, Shells, Macaroni,
    and Fusilli
De Boles
Multigrain Spaghetti
Rice Spirals
Felicia Bio® Buckwheat Gluten-Free Tortiglioni
Tolerant Brand®—Red Lentil Penne
Black Bean Penne
Mini Fettuccine
Black Bean Rotini
King Soba® Organic Black Rice Gluten-Free Noodles

Jovial® Organic Brown Rice Pasta—Lasagna, Fusilli, and Elbows
Explore Asian
Organic Aduki Bean Spaghetti
Organic Black Bean Spaghetti
Organic Mung Bean and
    Edamame Fettuccine Shape

Lundberg® Organic Brown Rice Pasta
Maple Groves® Brown Rice Spaghetti
Tinkyada® Brown Rice, Rice Bran Pastas
Fusilli
Fettucine
Spirals
Spinach Brown Rice Spaghetti
Shells
Lasagna
And more!

Truroots® Organic Ancient Grain Pasta
Quinoa and Amaranth, Brown Rice Pasta

Note: I haven't added white rice, Asian noodles, or bean thread noodles because they don't have much nutrition or flavor, but they are widely available. Also available are the "Miracle Noodles" made with psyllium husk. Look for them in Asian markets and in the Asian section of most grocery stores.

Fresh Gluten-free pastas in the refrigerated section:
Here's a short list, but ask your grocery clerk if they have any fresh gluten-free ravioli and pastas. Many of those are available regionally.
Delallo Gnocci
RP's Pasta Company

Gluten-Free Linguini
Gluten-Free Fusilli
Gluten-Free Fettuccine
Gluten-Free Lasagna Sheets
Gluten-Free Spinach Fettuccine

Resources:
Whole Grains Council: www.wholegrainscouncil.org
Celiac Disease: www.celiac.org
www.glutenfree.com

Index

Pistachio-Encrusted Shrimp with Black Mahogany Rice, 156, *157*

Red Yams with Black Rice and Goat Cheese, 148, *149*

Blueberry Betty's (Vegan), 114, *115*

Blueberry Pancakes with Amaranth, Quinoa, and Almond Flour, 6, *7*

Bob's Red Mill Gluten-Free 1 to 1 Baking Flour®, 130

Bob's Red Mill Gluten-free Baking Flour®, 4, 130

Bob's Red Mill Gluten-free Baking Powder, 120

Bob's Red Mill® Polenta Mix, 92, 152

Bragg's Liquid Aminos®, 52

Bread, banana, 122, *123*

Breakfast Hash with Sweet Peppers, Brussels Sprouts, Japanese Yams, and Sorghum, 20, *21*

Breakfast Lasagna with Vegetarian Chorizo Crumbles, 12, *13*

Breakfast Sage Burger with Bhutan Red Rice, Rainbow Chard, and Asiago Cheese, 18, *19*

Brownies
Gooey Chocolate Espresso Brownies, 130, *131*
Spicy Brownies, 120, *121*

Brown rice
Curried Garbanzo Beans with Eggplant and Brown Basmati Rice, 26, *27*
Fast and Savory Chicken Soup with Quinoa, Brown Rice, and Mushrooms, 50, *51*
Mexican Black Bean Stack with Vegetables, Red Quinoa, and Brown Rice, 102, *103*
Quick Stuffed Mushrooms with Quinoa and Brown Rice, Dates, and Goat Cheese, 158, *159*
Three Leaf Salad with Pistachios and Lemon Dressing, 30

Brown rice spiral pasta, 104

Brussels sprouts, Breakfast Hash with Sweet Peppers, Japanese Yams, and, 20, *21*

Buckwheat, x

Buffalo Chicken Flatbread Pizza, 78, *79*

Burger, Breakfast Sage, 18, *19*

Cabbage
Mexican Wrap with Chicken and Chipotle Hummus, 64, *65*
shredded cabbage slaw, 76
Spicy Black Bean Noodle Salad with Cabbage and Thai Peanut Salad, 32, *33*

Cakes
Chocolate Bundt Cake with Guajillo Pepper Spicy Sweet Frosting, 138, *139*
Coconut Flour Lemon and Coconut Cake, 134, *135*

Cannellini beans, Roasted Beet Salad with, 44, *45*

Carrots
Breakfast Sage Burger with Bhutan Red Rice, Rainbow Chard, and Asiago Cheese, 18, *19*
Roasted Carrots and Parsnips with Za'atar and Forbidden Rice, 52, *53*
Spicy Black Bean Noodle Salad with Cabbage and Thai Peanut Salad, 32, *33*

Vietnamese Salad with Grilled Shrimp and Purple Yam Noodles, 58, *59*

Zesty Kañiwa Salad with Roasted Vegetables and Basil Vinaigrette, 54, *55*

Cauliflower
Forbidden Rice Salad with Heirloom Carrots and Cauliflower, 38, *39*
Purple Cauliflower Pizza with Sundried Tomatoes and Cilantro Pesto, 68, *69*

Chanterelle mushrooms, 96

Chard
Breakfast Sage Burger with Bhutan Red Rice, Rainbow Chard, and Asiago Cheese, 18, *19*
Swiss Chard and Artichoke Salad with Cannellini Beans and Bhutan Red Rice, 48, *49*

Cheese
Breakfast Sage Burger with Bhutan Red Rice, Rainbow Chard, and Asiago Cheese, 18, *19*
Meatballs with Edamame Mung Bean Fettuccine and Pesto, 94, *95*
Polenta with Fire-Roasted Tomatoes with Green Chili and Cotija Cheese, 92, *93*
Polenta with Turkey, Harissa, and Feta Cheese, 152, *153*
Purple Cauliflower Pizza with Sundried Tomatoes and Cilantro Pesto, 68, *69*
Savory Corn and Cheese Muffins, 124, *125*
Tuna and Lemony Artichoke Pizza with Capers and Manchego Cheese, 70, 71

Cherry Almond Biscotti with Cocoa Nibs, 108, *109*

Cherry tomatoes. *See* Tomatoes (fresh)

Chicken
Almond-Crusted Chicken with Adzuki Bean Spaghetti, 90, *91*
Buffalo Chicken Flatbread Pizza, 78, *79*
Chicken Salad Wrap with Sumac-Herbed Black Rice, 80, *81*
Curried Flatbread with Chicken and Hot Curry Paste, 66, *67*
Fast and Savory Chicken Soup with Quinoa, Brown Rice, and Mushrooms, 50, *51*
Fast Chicken Wrap with Red Pepper Hummus, 74, *75*
Fast Open-Faced Mediterranean Wrap, 82, *83*
Hearty Southwestern Chicken Veggie Soup with Bean and Quinoa Pasta, 56, *57*
Mexican Wrap with Chicken and Chipotle Hummus, 64, *65*
Rustic Chicken with Asparagus, Sun-dried Tomatoes, and Mushrooms, 104, *105*
Spicy Mexican Chicken with Penne and Peppers, 98, *99*

Chicken andouille sausage, 100

Chicken Salad Wrap with Sumac-Herbed Black Rice, 80, *81*

Chickpeas
Breakfast Sage Burger with Bhutan Red Rice, Rainbow Chard, and Asiago Cheese, 18, *19*